KU-548-769

Born and raised in Portland, Maine, **Anna Kendrick** made her Broadway debut at the age of twelve in her Tony-nominated performance for the musical *High Society*. Since her Academy Award-nominated role as Natalie Keener in *Up in the Air*, she has made numerous theatrical appearances, including starring roles in *Into the Woods*, the *Twilight* saga and the *Pitch Perfect* film franchise. In 2013, she achieved musical success with the triple-platinum hit song 'Cups (When I'm Gone)', featured in *Pitch Perfect*. She lives in Los Angeles, California.

ANNA KENDRICK

scrappy little nobody

**SIMON &
SCHUSTER**

London · New York · Sydney · Toronto · New Delhi

A CBS COMPANY

First published in Great Britain by Simon & Schuster UK Ltd, 2016
This paperback edition published by Simon & Schuster UK Ltd, 2017
A CBS COMPANY

Copyright © 2016 by 207, INC.

Certain names and characteristics have been changed.

This book is copyright under the Berne Convention.
No reproduction without permission.
All rights reserved.

The right of Anna Kendrick to be identified as the author of this work has been
asserted by her in accordance with sections 77 and 78 of the Copyright,
Designs and Patents Act, 1988.

1 3 5 7 9 10 8 6 4 2

Simon & Schuster UK Ltd
1st Floor
222 Gray's Inn Road
London WC1X 8HB

www.simonandschuster.co.uk
www.simonandschuster.com.au
www.simonandschuster.co.in

Simon & Schuster Australia, Sydney
Simon & Schuster India, New Delhi

The author and publishers have made all reasonable efforts to contact
copyright-holders for permission, and apologise for any omissions or errors in
the form of credits given. Corrections may be made to future printings.

A CIP catalogue record for this book is available from the British Library.

Paperback ISBN: 978-1-4711-5683-0
eBook ISBN: 978-1-4711-5684-7

Printed and bound by CPI Group (UK) Ltd, Croydon, CR0 4YY

Interior design by Jill Putorti
Illustrations by Robin Eisenberg
Photograph on page 35 by Joan Marcus
Photograph on page 211 by Jeff Kravitz / FilmMagic / Getty Images

Simon & Schuster UK Ltd are committed to sourcing paper that is made from
wood grown in sustainable forests and support the Forest Stewardship Council, the
leading international forest certification organisation. Our books displaying the
FSC logo are printed on FSC certified paper.

To Mike,
watch out for the icy patch.

contents

HOLLYWOOD

SCRAPPY LITTLE NOBODY

author's note

I'm sure I've mixed up the timeline and contradicted myself, but I've tried to get it right. I've changed some names to protect the innocent—and to protect my mother from people in her book club coming at her like, "That's not how *my* kid remembers that day in preschool." A lot of things that are meaningful to me didn't make the cut because they just weren't entertaining. For example, my childhood best friend Meg isn't in the book at all because it turns out my mom was right: those stories really are only funny to the two of us.

introduction

1. braid hair
2. arrange books by color
3. do homework on the floor
4. feng shui room
5. magazine collage
6. lie in yard with Walkman

When I was thirteen I started making lists. I've always liked structure, and I thought if I broke it down into steps, I could will myself to fit in. My idea of "normal" came mainly from film and television, and with that as my guide, I wrote down the kinds of things a "normal" girl might be doing when a boy showed up unexpectedly at her house. Of course, the one time a boy showed up unexpectedly at *my* house, he found this list.

Jared was one of the popular kids at school. We weren't close, but he was a neighbor, so he occasionally came by. This was the only time he'd ever arrived unannounced. He spotted my notebook, opened it, and started reading out loud.

"Oh god, that's stupid. Seriously, put that down, it's nothing." I was in a full-out panic. *Come on, Anna, why would you generate written evidence of your social and emotional ineptitude and leave it lying around?*

As soon as he left, I ripped the pages out of my journal and burned them in the bathroom sink. The fire made the house stink of carbon for days. When my mom and dad came home I told them I'd been burning incense. I doubt my parents believed me, but they could sense my desperate need to drop the issue, so they moved on. That night, I resolved to keep the crazy inside my head where it belonged. Forever. But here's the thing about crazy: It. Wants. Out.

Once I'd moved out of the house at seventeen and there was less threat of unwanted guests pawing through my belongings, I attempted to keep a journal again. I managed only about a dozen entries over a period of two years, but I never did burn it.

Last year I found this journal. My handwriting as an angsty teen was appalling, yet somehow *better* than it is now. And the subject to which I devoted the most pages (besides my virginity) was the fear that I would fail—in all things—and have to go back home to Maine with my tail between my legs.

I had thought my younger self assumed everything would work out—that I was possessed of some reckless confidence you only have in youth. Otherwise, how could I have been fool enough to try? But the journal wasn't quixotic, it was fearful. The terror was so present, yet I was doing it anyway.

Shit, I thought, *I used to be tough. I used to be brave. I used to be a better version of me.* Lately I can't paint my bedroom walls without asking ten people for their opinion and eventually talking myself out of it altogether.

I'd moved away from everything I knew and loved at seventeen in spite of how scared I was. I wondered if I would still have it in me to do something I found so daunting. Aren't you supposed to get more independent as you get older? Shouldn't I be bolder, more self-sufficient? Have I gotten comfortable? Have I stopped pushing myself the way I did when I was trying to "make something of myself"? Was that a fluke?

I texted my brother.

Me: I miss being a scrappy little nobody. I was much more capable.

Mike: Dude.

Mike: You're still scrappy. You just get a lot more emails now.

Mike: P.S.

Mike: You're still a little nobody to me.*

As if I had asked the universe to send me an example of something intimidating—a test to see if I still had some nerve—the opportunity arose to write a book. Sure, it will be hard, but all you need to be a writer is perseverance, a low-level alcohol dependency, and a questionable moral compass. Is that not what

---

* Okay, he didn't actually say that last part, but it would have been perfect if he did.

you need? Well, I've got a bunch of embarrassing stories. And I'll keep the rest of that stuff in my back pocket.

Thanks to my old friend Jared, I'm a pretty private person. I never let anyone, not even friends, into my bedroom or my purse. I have a small stroke anytime someone asks to use my laptop; I only use that thing to look for porn and the definitions of words I should already know. Yet I've chosen to commit intimate details of my life and psyche to the page. So, step into my brain, kids!

I wish I could have called this "It's not that serious" or "A tweet, but longer." So much significance is placed on something you put in a book, and I don't care much for significance. Let's agree now that we're just having a conversation and I happen to talk more than I listen (true in real life as well). I tend to spew my opinions until someone interrupts me, and weirdly, my computer never gained sentience to save me from myself.

There were actually several stories that my mother specifically asked me to include—mostly those rare instances in which I did something out of generosity or love or some other motivation found in emotionally normative humans. I suspect she worries I'm too abrasive and wants me to provide some indication that I'm not a terrible person. Alas, I've tried to be honest, because honesty makes me feel less alone, and I hope you are entertained.

Maybe I should have learned my lesson about "written evidence." It's possible that in ten years, every word in here will send me into fits of humiliated paralysis. But the crazy wants out. Let's do this.

a few disclaimers

I'm Not Kool

Jessica was the first person to mistake me for someone cool.

When I was in kindergarten, both of my parents worked full-time, so I went to an after-school program. Every day, a van picked up a few kids from my class and made stops at local schools around the city before driving us to the YMCA in downtown Portland, Maine.

I had recently discovered (thanks to an incident my mother and father just *love* to recount) that I did not make a good first impression. Over the summer, we'd been to a family campground, and while other children met and became immediate playmates, that power evaded me. I sulked for the better part of a week and eventually asked my parents, "Will you find me a friend?" I don't get why that's so funny. That's basically how I feel as an adult. Will one of you guys find me a friend?

When we picked up Jessica from her school, she marched to the very back of the van—one row behind me—and tapped me on the shoulder. For a five-year-old, she was a deeply confident girl. Jessica was ready to judge her fellow passengers.

"Are you friends with anyone else here?" she asked.

My animal instincts knew she was The Alpha, and I needed to think fast to impress her.

"Oh," I said, "Dan . . . in the front seat. I know him."

I'd "known" Dan since eight o'clock that morning, but admitting I was friendless seemed like it would be worse than lying, so I took the risk. Then I had a terrifying thought: *What if she talks to Dan next?*

I continued. "I know Dan, but . . ." I leaned in. "He's kind of weird."

"Oooh." She nodded her head in recognition. Being judgmental was really taking me places. She narrowed her eyes. "We won't play with him." *If you say so, Jessica! Your alpha energy is making me feel alive!*

More kids got in the van and Jessica made her assessments swiftly. By the time we arrived, she had curated a small group of girls she deemed worthy and said, "We're going to play together. We're the cool kids club." *Hold up, Jess—I'm in the cool kids club?* I was five years old, but I already knew that wasn't right. *Just hang in there, Kendrick. Don't mess this up!*

The group decided we'd officially call ourselves the Cool Kids Club. Since kindergartners are so pressed for time, we decided to just use the initials. And since kindergartners are *excellent* at spelling, we called ourselves the KKK. When I proudly announced my new affiliation to my mother, she scrambled to explain that neither "Cool" nor "Club" starts with *K*, but I'd seen billboards for Kool cigarettes, so she wasn't fooling me.

The next day, during outside playtime at the Y, Jessica walked straight up to Dan and yelled, "We're not going to play with you!" She stomped off dramatically and took the rest of the girls with her.

What the hell was that, Jessica? I said the kid was "kind of weird," I didn't say he dismembered cats. You were only supposed to avoid him long enough that I wouldn't be caught in my lie!

Jessica became my first enemy. Like most enemies in my life, I hoped to punish her with passive-aggressive glances and silent—but passionate!—resentment. She retaliated by forgetting I existed. Ah, the moral victory.

I Am a Very, Very Small Weirdo

First grade was when I realized I was small. I was the smallest, youngest-looking child in every group, no matter the situation. In fact, this is something to bear in mind as we go. Whatever age I am in a given story, subtract three to four years and that's what I looked like.*

We were learning about outer space, and our teacher brought in a chart that told us what we would weigh on all the different planets. We were so excited to find out how crazy heavy we'd be on Jupiter and how crazy light we'd be on Pluto. My weight wasn't listed. It became clear that I didn't make the cut because there was no calculation for what I would weigh on Pluto. I

---

* Except when I was born. My god, I was so fat. I almost killed my mother. And while that's gross, it's completely true. If we lived in a time before cesarean sections, she wouldn't have survived. (I would also like to thank cesarean sections for sparing me the mental anguish of knowing I once passed through my mother's vaginal canal.)

would weigh nothing. Less than nothing. I would drift into space.

Oh man. I wasn't just the smallest one in the class; I was a freak. There was no metric for how deformed I was. It was one thing to be the Chihuahua in a group of Labradors; it was quite another to be the hamster.

That night I cried to my mother, who assured me that she had been small at my age, too.

Wow, that really doesn't help me right now, Mom. When I calmed down, I saw her point. She'd turned out fine. She wasn't living in a special community for the physically repulsive, so I decided I could go back to school the next day.

Even adults thought I was younger than I was. This made me extra sensitive, and though they may have meant well, I became one of those little kids who didn't enjoy grown-ups fucking with me.

One summer, a Russian wrestling team came through my hometown. My dad had been a wrestler in college, and I believe he was a bit starstruck. He took me to watch their first match, and after letting me play "imagination" under the bleachers for a few hours, he pushed me at the imposing coach, an absolute caricature of a man.

The coach eyed me and asked, "Vhat's your name, little guirl?"

"Anna."

"Ah. Anya!"

Foreigners, I stewed.

"No." I spoke more slowly this time. "Anna."

"Yes, Anya!"

Oh, this motherfucker thinks this is cute, I realized. *He thinks we're playing a little game.*

"It's ANNA," I said, and I put on my most fearsome face.

"Aw, Anya." He reached down and ruffled my hair.

I snapped my head around to face my dad. *Are you going to let him get away with this? This is the name of your beloved mother— may she rest in peace—which means that this man, this Russki, is making a mockery of your flesh and blood twofold!*

He noticed that I was on the verge of a tantrum and picked me up. "I think she's a little tired." *Oh, is that right?* And so I saw. I was going to have to fight and claw to be taken seriously in this life. And probably never quite succeed. I still try to be serious, but apathy has become a part of me now in a way that my six-year-old self couldn't have foreseen. I've never been able to muster the righteous indignation of my elementary school years.

Back at school, I tried to embrace the smallest things in every category. Favorite instrument in the orchestra? The piccolo. Favorite mammal? The shrew. Favorite country? Monaco. And my favorite planet? Pluto. (Screw you, Neil deGrasse Tyson.)

Always being the smallest also gave me a specific role in life; it gave me an identity. Lining up by height? Excuse me while I give you a starting point. Gymnastics day in gym class? I'll prepare myself to be thrown.

On one "family cleaning" day, my dad bought an extendable duster to clean under low tables, and I lost my mind because I thought I no longer had a purpose in the family. He threw away the duster and went back to letting me do a mediocre job crawling under the furniture.

First grade led to other discoveries, too. I was small, I was loud, I had ratty hair, but I suspected something deeper was wrong. One day, I tried to articulate this suspicion to my mother.

"It's like, it's like I have a different heart. The other girls have one kind of heart, and I have a different kind."

My mom was understandably confused. "Are you saying they're mean?"

"No . . . I don't know."

Saying other kids were mean felt like I was saying I was more kind, which definitely wasn't it—more anxious maybe, more sensitive. I guess all I was feeling was that I was different.

Sometimes I'll be at work or a party and get that same feeling. *I am not like these people. I don't know what I'm doing here.* And it comforts me to know that I felt that way as a child, too. Maybe that should make me feel worse, but it makes me calm and resolved. I've been prepared to be an outsider most of my life.

I Remember Every Slight: You've Been Warned

In fourth grade I managed to get a good thing going when I discovered the secret to female bonding: the sleepover. Six girls from school would come over to my house and we'd roll out sleeping bags in the spare bedroom above the garage. This became a regular thing, and for the first time I felt like I had a steady group of friends. Even if my attempts at social interaction throughout the school week became awkward and tiresome, by Friday it was sleepover time again and all was forgiven.

One weekend I went out of town for a dance recital, and when I came back I was informed that a sleepover had taken place without me. Apparently, since my house hadn't been an option, Tori had offered to host.

Tori wasn't in the group, but she'd seen her opportunity to usurp me and she took it. I didn't like Tori; Tori was mean. If I'd known what was good for me, I would have just shut up and accepted that we could alternate weekends. Maybe I'd even have to invite her over from now on, but that would be a small price to pay for true friendship. Sadly, my sense of justice would not allow me to make this sacrifice; I'd rather be right than happy. I reminded the girls that we, as a group, didn't *like* Tori, that she was a bully. But no one listened.

The next day on the playground I was standing in line for the monkey bars, thinking about what I would say if I ever met the cast of *Boy Meets World*, and then I was on the ground. Fuzzy black stars appeared and dissolved in slow motion, and when my vision came back, I felt a choking sensation. I was being dragged across the gravel by the collar of my army jacket.

Tori!

I scratched and clawed at her, but she was big for our grade. She towed me across the playground and under the slide. When I was put on my feet, I stood in front of a tribunal of the sleepover gang, who were standing in over-the-top indignant poses.

The slide on this particular playground was flanked by a wooden climbing wall (a normal wall with an old rope on it), so when you were underneath it you had a degree of privacy. Students had taken to scratching their initials into the backside of The Wall's soft wood, which gave this dark corner of the playground a kind of menacing, Victorian-asylum quality. Something new was there. Haphazardly written in some kind of Magic Marker were the words *Mary D is a jerk*. In fact, as my eyes began to adjust, I saw that hastily scrawled insults about almost every girl in our group now adorned The Wall. Based on the manner in which I'd been summoned to this meeting, I knew what was coming.

I tried to protest. I didn't do it! I was their friend! I mean, *"Mary D is a jerk"*? *"Amanda sucks"*? Why would I write a bunch of mean stuff about my friends?! Using such generic insults?!

I noticed how high the writing was placed and rushed toward The Wall to demonstrate that I couldn't have done it! I wasn't even tall enough! Surely they could see that! Once I started to reach my arm up, though, it looked like I would be able to make it if I got up on my toes. I made a big show of flailing my hand just beneath the writing but kept my heels firmly on the ground, as though I was the kind of person who couldn't balance otherwise.

This was a setup. I suggested alternative suspects, I tried to look as outraged for my friends as they were themselves. I *knew* it was Tori; it was so obvious I couldn't believe I'd even have to say it. But she was tall and I was outnumbered, so I wasn't about to accuse her then and there.

Once we were back in the classroom and under the safety of adult supervision, I made the rounds to each girl. I whispered that it *had* to be Tori, that she was trying to squeeze me out, that they were giving her exactly what she wanted! Sadly, by this time, they were enjoying their dramatic game of cold-shoulder too much. It would have spoiled their fun to stop hating me.

The next day I regrouped. Sure, I was starting to hate them right back, but I'd been wronged and this would not stand. I doubled down on the "too short" angle, took a ruler outside at recess, and recorded the results. The measurements were shoddy, but what my evidence lacked in accuracy I made up for in volume. That's how you save a friendship: comprehensive documentation!

I also pointed out that defacing property was not in my nature. I'd read about the disappearing beaches in *National Geographic Kids* and my anxiety about the environment went through the roof, so I did *not* condone waste, littering, or "graffiti." I even argued that the use of the word "suck" should have eliminated me from suspicion, because I was against swearing. (Oh, sweet, naive younger me.)

They would not be moved. The harder I tried to prove my innocence the more I revealed my true nature, and eventually their motivation for shunning me transformed. It became less about the alleged betrayal and more about their aversion to hyperactive little weirdos. They'd moved on from being angry and settled into just not liking me.

This is how supervillains are created.

origin story

There was a small window in my early childhood when I wanted to be a doctor. This was inspired by my pediatrician, a relatively young man whom I called Dr. Handsome. I had assumed this was because his name was Dr. Hasen or Dr. Branson, but I recently found out his name was Dr. Ritger, so I guess I should have just died at age four when I decided to call my physician Dr. Handsome without so much as a pun to justify it. Anyway, I

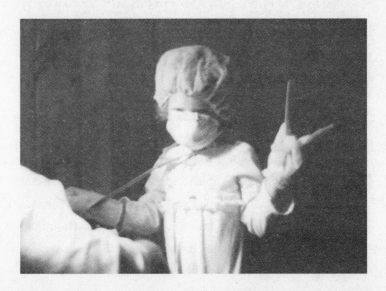

loved Dr. Handsome. All I actually knew about him was that he was nice and he helped people, but he got a lot of attention for it, which seemed like a pretty sweet gig.

"When I grow up, I'm going to be a poor doctor," I announced. My mom asked me what I meant.

"I'm going to be a doctor for poor people," I said. "They won't need to pay, I'll work for free." My mom is a sucker for this kind of sweet-little-kid stuff, but she had to point out that I might face complications in adult life, even if it meant crushing my dream.

"That's very nice, sweetheart, but if you work for free, what will you do for money?" My mom was an accountant and the breadwinner in the family. Teaching her children about money was the responsible thing to do. She may have even wondered if my brother or I would follow in her footsteps.

I thought about this for a while. I'd just been served a heavy dose of reality.

"Oh!" I said. *I can't believe you didn't think of this yourself, Mom.* "If I run out of money, I'll just write a check." She knew then that a career in finance was not for me.

Aside from becoming Martyr, MD, I didn't have many career goals before I decided I wanted to perform. Sometimes this worries me. Am I like one of those Chinese gymnasts who's known nothing but this life, never able to consider another option? Am I going to wake up in ten years and say, "Someone get me to a lab; I've got some shit to discover!" I would actually love that. Having zero education to back up the desire would be irritating, but going to college at forty with a background in the arts and discovering the competitive world of science would be . . . a terrible movie! Terrible screenplay idea number one! (Terrible title ideas include but are not limited to: *The Science of Art*! *The Art of Science*! *Old Maid in a Lab Coat*!)

Still, performing is all I've cared about since the first time I can remember caring about anything. I don't know how you pursue acting as an adult. It's possible that the process would have subjected me to more discouraging situations than I could handle and I would have bailed and started a closet-organizing business . . . while letting my OWN life and home fall into chaos! Terrible screenplay idea number two! (Terrible title ideas include but are not limited to: *Closet Case*! *Organize This*! *Mothballs and Heartbreak*! *Love Hoarder*!) I'm glad I got started early.

It's All Mike's Fault

There are plenty of early influences I could point to—*Newsies*, *Life with Mikey*, everything Bette Midler ever did—but my brother, Mike, claims I started performing because I wanted to copy him. Which is absolutely true.

My brother is my hero. I've idolized him since the day I was born, and I still do. He's responsible for at least sixty percent of my personality, for better or worse. I'm told that if you're an only child, you grow up thinking you're the center of the universe, and if you have tons of siblings you grow up with a healthy perspective on how small you are in the grand scheme of things. I'd like to think that my brother told me I was a worthless brat often enough that I got the same effect.

Not having it.

Our dad had been an athlete in college and exposed the two of us to every team sport Maine had to offer. The poor man got so excited whenever we showed the slightest aptitude for sports, only to have his hopes dashed when we gave them up just as quickly. The summer I played T-ball, I got in trouble for blowing kisses to my friend Margaret Eddy, the first baseman for the other team. Soccer didn't appeal to me at all. I stood still in the middle of the field for the entirety of the one game I played. The other kids had the ball, I'd wait my turn. Most important, my brother had no real interest in sports, and I wasn't about to waste my time doing something where I couldn't follow him around.

Mike's main interests were watching *Star Wars*, playing Magic: The Gathering, and avoiding his annoying little sister. The only time he happily included me was when he wanted to play "Pro

Wrestling Champions," as I was an ideal partner on whom to inflict moderate injury.

At a certain point he realized that I was sticking around (no matter how often he told me I was adopted and should run away). He reluctantly accepted that he would have to put up with my pestering questions and should probably try to ameliorate my lameness in the process. I asked him what Cypress Hill meant by "Tell Bill Clinton to go and inhale" and he rolled his eyes and made the international sign for "smoking weed" by pressing his thumb and forefinger to his lips. I nodded like I understood, which I did not. Two years later I asked him what Alanis Morissette meant by "go down on you in a theater." He let out a sigh that communicated, *You're such a loser wanting to know this stuff and you're an even bigger loser for not knowing already*, and then made the international sign for "blow job" by pumping his fist in front of his mouth and pulling a slack-jawed, idiotic expression. You know, like all girls do when they're giving a blow job. I nodded like I understood, which again I did not.

He protected me, too. When I was ten, our dentist needed to take impressions of my teeth. To do this, the bored dental hygienist stuck a mold in my mouth that felt like it was the size of a grapefruit and told me to stay still for about two minutes. I tried, using hand signals, to protest that I was about to choke and die. She rolled her eyes and told me to breathe through my nose. When I vomited all over the station she started screaming at me, but at least she took out the mold and I could draw enough breath to start crying. Mike was having his checkup in the next room and rushed over to me. Then my twelve-year-old brother marched out and told our dentist that he was going to kill him.

Deep down, he loves me.

When we were really little Mike showed me a neat trick that he called "Drama." He screamed as loud as he could and when our babysitter ran into the room in a panic, he said, "Just drama." And thus, the seed was planted.

When he was seven I followed his lead again. Mike enrolled in dance classes because he wanted to learn to "rap dance," which probably meant however Vanilla Ice was dancing. After his first lesson, he came home in a pair of baggy pants with a geometric neon pattern, knowing how to do the running man. For the first time, I knew the cold sting of being the biggest loser on the planet.

I cried to my parents that I wanted to take dance lessons, too. My parents were bona fide masters of letting us think we were in control, especially when it came to keeping the peace between my brother and me. They presented me with the option of taking tap and ballet, which meant prettier costumes, and I agreed that hip-hop class with a bunch of boys did not sound like the best fit for me. Had it not been for Mike and Vanilla Ice and those baggy neon pants, I might never have discovered my calling.

Little Orphan Anna

At five, I had a plump face and dirty-blond curls, and people would often tell my parents that I looked like Shirley Temple. I knew nothing about Shirley Temple, but she's like me, you say? Well, she must be marvelous! I adore Shirley Temple! My dance teacher said the same thing when I started classes with her, and once I revealed my secret power to grind dance class to a halt by randomly singing at the top of my lungs, she suggested that I sing the Shirley Temple classic "On the Good Ship Lollipop" at the recital. Tap, ballet, AND a solo performance?! I was stretched so thin, but my public demanded it.

(Incidentally, Shirley Temple made like seven movies at the age of six, which is straight-up child abuse, but kind of badass.)

The recital was just your run-of-the-mill clusterfuck—children screaming and running around backstage at a local high school auditorium. My big number was going brilliantly until halfway through the second verse, when I got to the bit about landing in a chocolate bar. It was my favorite part, and I gave

Moments before disaster.

that mediocre piece of wordplay the kind of hammy treatment that would have made the overworked Ms. Temple proud. Lesson: if you start congratulating yourself mid-performance, you are about to screw up.

I forgot the next lyrics. I stood onstage with my mouth open while the adults in the front row tried to get me back on track. I weighed my options, and while it didn't occur to me to simply *leave the stage*, I devised this impromptu exit strategy: slowly slide my feet farther and farther apart, then let gravity take over until I eventually face-plant in slow motion on the stage. I hoped I would wake up in bed. I hoped someone would come scoop me up and take me to Dunkin' Donuts. But that didn't happen. The prerecorded accompaniment did not stop. After a while I sat back up, and when the chorus came back around, I started singing again, red-faced and with far less conviction. The song ended and I walked offstage to where my mom was waiting for me. I said, "Well, that was stupid."

My mom tells this story with affection. I suppose that's because I shook it off. I didn't say I wanted to quit and I wasn't afraid to show my face after messing up. She probably should have been a *little* worried about that reaction, though. What a little sociopath, right?

The following year, in spite of my disastrous debut performance, my dance teacher suggested that I audition for some local theater. Our community theater was run-down but very charming, and they were about to put on a production of *Annie*, which is going to come up a lot in my childhood. My apologies.

In preparation, I watched the 1982 film version of *Annie*

with my family and my world exploded. These girls were dancing, singing, causing trouble, and playing with dogs—I needed this to be my life. I was too young to play Annie, but I wanted the part of Molly desperately. Molly is the young orphan whom Annie comforts with the song "Maybe." It's a pretty heartbreaking piece of music, and I wanted to get in there and chew some of that depressing scenery.

Alas, they went in a different direction for Molly, but I got to play Tessie. The internet informs me that Tessie is ten years old, while Molly is six, but in our version Tessie was "the littlest orphan." Tacking on any superlative is a surefire way to get a kid excited about something, so it was a clever way to convince me that Tessie was a special character. However, Tessie *should* be the littlest orphan. What kind of ten-year-old has a catchphrase like "Oh my goodness, oh my goodness! They're fightin' and I won't get no sleep all night!" Get your shit together, Tessie.

Doing the show was the best. I was in heaven. Being tiny was a good thing, being loud was a good thing. In everything else I'd done in my six years on earth, I'd been told I had too much energy, but here, I had somewhere to channel it all! We sang "It's the Hard-Knock Life"! We did a dance with tin buckets and scrub brushes that was bursting with adorable scrappy rage! We got to embody the rollicking fun of being orphans! (Why are kids so obsessed with orphans?) We got to play with a dog!! At one point the director told the girls we were playing too rough with the dog and they should play with me instead, because it might tire me out a little. So maybe I still had too much energy—they're adding a TAP number?! Let's go learn it!

To this day, seeing a tattered brown cardigan or a pair of thin-soled lace-up boots makes my heart sing. In a costume context, not, like, on a person. I'm not some out-of-touch monster who sees real-world poverty and longs for the days of her musical-theater beginnings.

One review mentioned me. The reviewer said something nice but remarkably unspecific, yet my mother and father know that sentence verbatim to this day. I won't bother pretending that I think that's lame of them (I mean, it is, I just don't *think* it is), because having my parents love and support me is a pretty sweet situation, as parent-child relationships go.

My next local gig was playing Baby June in a production of *Gypsy* a few towns away. The director was a woman with enormous black hair who seemed to bathe in knockoff Chanel No. 5 and tacky jewelry. I'd never met someone who was so unapologetic about how they looked. She sparkled like a Christmas disco ball at all times. If I'd known what a drag queen was, I would have thought, *That woman looks like a female drag queen* and chuckled to myself about my very first piece of lazy observational humor. Instead I thought, *That woman is all the colors of the rainbow and I want to roll around in her closet.*

She turned out to be all business when it came to this production, and, no, I would NOT be allowed to use a trick baton, I would learn to twirl the batons, because that's what professionals do! And don't put your hand there, put it two centimeters to the left! And learn right from left, Anna! The day I cried because I realized that Dainty June (the slightly older version of my character) was played by a different actress, she said, "Yes, that's right, so let's rehearse the transition number again. Dig your own grave, little one." Okay, she didn't say the "dig your own grave" part, but she was not sympathetic.

With our ruthless and bejeweled director at the helm, the Biddeford City Theater production of *Gypsy* was actually pretty good. Looking back, I've wondered why she was so demanding. It was just community theater. Why did it have to be so perfect? But I've also now been around enough people who have a low opinion of anyone who is creative in a nonprofessional realm to know that that's ugly and ignorant. People don't have to do things by half measures because they aren't getting paid for it. In fact, that's all the more reason to throw every ounce of passion you have behind it. I think she could have yelled a bit less for the sensitive types like me who need to be told they are wonderful every half hour to accomplish anything at all, but I respect that she pushed herself and everyone around her.

The show paired me with an onstage sister, a.k.a. MY DE-FAULT NEW BEST FRIEND! Virginia was an unsuspecting tomboy with maybe eight months on me, which was a lifetime of experience. She was unaware that we were going to be best friends, but after a while I wore her down and she introduced me to the excitement of the occult! The theater we were in was a beautiful 1890s opera house, and we played with a Ouija board in the balcony between rehearsals. She told me stories about Helen, the ghost that haunted the theater, and how if we played with the Ouija board too often, Satan would have enough power to bring Helen back from the dead to destroy us all. Kids are dark.

We stayed in touch for a while after the show, mostly because Virginia was very excited about becoming someone's pen pal. At her suggestion, we promised to write each other letters, and as the show came to a close, she began to add more and more detail to her plan for our epistolary adventures. She said we could enclose small items like "beads we find" and smear the paper with our current favorite lipstick and circle it to ask, "What do you think of this shade?" The level of specificity rattled me.

Even at eight, I could tell that this was a contrivance based on something she had read in a book or seen in a movie. In her first letter to me, I found a handful of beads and a smear of lipstick. I still enjoyed the letters and tried to participate in the suggested spirit of her requests without doing exactly what she'd described. I sent her shells from the beach by my grandparents' house and pictures I cut out of magazines. She sent her next letter with nothing inside, and we volleyed for a few more weeks until it petered out. Don't try to participate in anyone else's idea of what is supposed to happen in a relationship. You will fail.

The show also introduced a dangerous new concept to my family. *Gypsy* and the main character of Mama Rose explore the effects of the "stage parent" on both child and mother. My parents immediately saw in Mama Rose a blueprint of everything they wanted to avoid. We hadn't met any stage parents in real life yet, but if I was going to be playing around with this theater thing for a year or two (little did they know), no one in my family was going to push anyone into doing anything, and for the next decade my parents went on high alert for signs that I wanted to stop. (I think they might still be waiting. Maybe that's why my mom is always telling me she loves me because I'm a good person or whatever.)

Early Bird

I get embarrassed about being a "child actor." Probably because I spent a lot of time around child actors when I was one. They're crazy. When people ask me how I got started, I'll usually make some crack about how I was one of those "freaky kid actors," and how "all that's missing is the drug problem." I want to get in front of the story so I can control it! Maybe people don't have judgmental feelings about child actors. I just worry that it conjures images of pushy parents, or tiny diva hissy fits, or *Star Search*. Okay, I did audition for *Star Search*, but I didn't get on the show, so I hope you're happy.

At ten, I stood in a modest office in Manhattan and sang "Tomorrow" from *Annie* (I warned you) for a children's talent agent. That was basically it. That was all I had to do. That, and cry in the lobby beforehand, because I got nervous and my mom had to remind me that my cousin Tina wasn't going to get married thirty minutes from New York City every weekend.

When I first moved to Los Angeles, occasionally a friend who was struggling would ask me how I got my agent, and telling this story always made me feel like a lucky little jackass. I would try to make the story funny, like I didn't know they were hoping to glean some actionable piece of wisdom out of it. The truth is, I had nothing to offer in the way of advice. Cold-call a talent agent? But first, be ten years old?

At that age, I didn't have a résumé, but I wasn't expected to. At ten, I had a big voice that stood in exponential contrast to my size. I could learn a melody. I didn't sound like a dying cat.

I was not one of those kids who started young and never stopped working—there are many pathetic tales in these pages to prove it. But I'm glad I got my foot in the door at an age when some of the scariest people had to take it easy on me, because I was Just A Kid. If you are expecting to find advice, I will be no help at all. I have no advice. I do have a truckload of opinions, which I will happily prattle on about to anyone who gives me an opening. I'd just like to add the "for entertainment purposes only" disclaimer to everything in here, like I'm a psychic hotline or a bot on AshleyMadison.com.

I don't know what my parents anticipated happening once I got a fancy agent four states away. Maybe they knew that supporting the larger dream while I was a kid was easier than praying it was a phase and begrudgingly supporting me later on. Maybe they only hoped I would book a commercial and get the kind of money that starts a solid college fund in one swoop. That would have been fine with me—I couldn't differentiate between the prestige of a Broadway show and a regional commercial, so I would have been just as happy about becoming an underage corporate stooge.

The agency that took me on lined up a few auditions for Broadway shows—the very first one was for *Annie* (I don't know what to tell you guys, it's just what happened). Then they lined up a handful of commercial auditions. My first auditions for commercials were weird. As were all the ones that would follow.

Commercial casting directors were looking for either pre-ternaturally beautiful children or children who were willing to cheese it up so hard they went blue in the face. At that age, I never thought about being pretty. That's not because I was enlightened, it's because I was a little kid and "pretty" seemed like adult criteria. (I did think about whether or not I would GROW UP to be pretty—all the time. I asked to see pictures of my grandmother as a young woman, I asked to see pictures of my mother as a young woman. I found out my mother's side of the family was universally flat-chested, so I asked if my *deceased* paternal grandmother had anything better goin' on back in the day. I was a ladylike and sensitive child.)

As for the cheese factor, I was no better off. This was the origin of my aversion to child actors. Most of them were fucking weirdos—a bunch of precocious extroverts who were learning to kiss adults' asses and say things like "How old do you want me to be?" I was a loud, hyperactive loser, but I was self-aware enough to know that would make me look like a dick.

Perhaps because my family's emotional range spanned from composed to stoic, I was not trying to play ball. For all the trouble I'd been in in my life for having "too much energy," I could not figure out why I was supposed to be so excited about tangle-free shampoo. My hair was always tangled and I was doing just fine, thank you very much.

Kids in these audition waiting rooms were unlike anything I'd seen before. They would make a big show of running up to other kids they knew and say things like "I haven't seen you since we outgrew the *Music Man* tour!" They would humble-brag about the last commercial they'd booked or how they'd screen-tested for a TV pilot last week, and their sleazy managers would say, "Our little Portia is a booking machine!"

Usually my mom or my dad was with me in these waiting rooms. My mom was always kind and wonderful, but, like me, my mom is a people pleaser and a rule follower. We were at a professional audition; I would go in with my headshot and résumé and try my best, and she would be the supportive parent who accompanies (but does not pressure!) her child.

My dad had far less patience. He was my stoic life vest. He's the smartest person I know. Not the smartest person I've ever met (I've met Dr. Oz and Dakota Fanning) but the smartest person I can call on the phone. He's an incredible resource but also very frustrating. It's like having Stephen Fry for a father. He makes you feel like an idiot just by breathing.

Like my mom, he wanted to make his children feel loved and wanted, but he's almost painfully Irish, so repression is more in his wheelhouse. The only time I've ever seen him cry was when he described the plot of the film *Rudy* to me. The unnerving thing was that I didn't even realize he was crying for ten minutes. At first, it just seemed like he had allergies or he'd eaten some spicy food. Aside from the tears, there was no other indication that he was emotional.

Sometimes I'd sit there, surrounded by kids loudly going over their one line of dialogue with parents chatting about which voice coach they were going to use now that Mrs. Ulanova had taken on too many students and wasn't giving little Teresa the kind of personalized attention she really needed to flourish, and

I'd feel myself start to spiral. I wouldn't just wonder if I belonged there, I'd descend into big-question territory. *Is this what everyone outside of Maine is like? Is this what the future will be like? Is this what actors are like? Is this what I'm like?*

I would turn my head maybe fifteen degrees and my dad would be staring straight ahead, and then, as if he'd been waiting for me, he'd throw me a look. *These people are freaks; let's get this over with, get the hell out of here, and get a Hostess Cupcake from the rest stop on the way home.* It felt like coming up for air.

It only took a few months before my agent mercifully realized that I sucked at commercial auditions. They decided I should start coming in only for theater, which made me very happy. Not because as a ten-year-old from Maine with no experience I thought I was too good for anything, but because professional auditions were in New York, which meant that one of my parents had to take time off work, drive me six hours to the city for an audition that usually lasted ten minutes, and then drive me six hours back. Yes, you are correct, what my parents did for me was crazy and I'll never be able to repay them as long as I live.

I had my first successful audition at age twelve for a musical called *High Society*, although when I arrived I assumed it wasn't going to go well. In the waiting room, I was struck by the uniformity of dress. The character was from a rich family, and my competitors looked the part. How did a girl age ten to fourteen even come by a sweater set? Weren't those available exclusively to toddlers and women over sixty?

The audition room was long and mirrored and had creaky wooden floors. I gave my sheet music to the pianist in the corner and turned to face a small row of people sitting behind a folding table at the far end of the room.

"Whoa, whoa. Let me look at your nails, young lady." Legendary casting director Jay Binder, who would become my greatest champion, was motioning me forward.

My nails were forest green with gold stars, which was pretty unusual, especially on a child in the days before Pinterest-chic nail art. I walked up to show him, unsure if I was in trouble or about to be told how wonderful I was.

"I got them done in Florida. I was visiting my grandparents for Thanksgiving and my mom took me to a nail place."

"Your mother let you get green nails?"

I nodded.

"Pretty cool mom. All right, what are you gonna sing for us, honey?"

I walked back to the center of the room with a great gift. Jay Binder had said, *Come up here, we're not scary; we want you to do well, cute nails, now please go do something impressive.* Almost every audition that has gone well in my life started with something like this. A week later, I was told to come back and audition for the director and producers.

Mike and Anna Take New York

As supportive as they were, my parents were looking for a way to get me to New York without relying on them for transportation since they enjoyed having jobs and paying bills and other accoutrements of middle-class survival. By this time, my brother was fourteen and they deemed him perfectly capable of accompanying his twelve-year-old sister on a bus to New York. So that's what we started doing.

People who grew up in major cities may wonder why the hell I would act like it's a big deal to be unaccompanied in New York City at that age: it's populated with both adults and children, it's a functioning metropolis, Kevin McCallister was only ten in *Home Alone 2: Lost in New York*, and *that* kid saved Christmas. Conversely, people from suburban areas act like my parents sent me wandering around the site of the Baby Jessica well, blindfolded and holding a flaming baton. So pick a side and prepare to judge me either way!

My parents bought a couple of bus tickets, and my brother and I got ready for our day trip. We packed extra batteries for our Walkmen, the family cell phone "for emergencies," two Lunchables, and this time—drumroll!—I wore a cardigan. I was gonna totally look the part. The one cardigan I owned was chunky and black with a jewel-toned pattern that looked so much like jet fighters from the Star Wars universe, I referred to it as my X-Wing sweater. I paired it with wide-leg jeans and black lace-up boots with thick rubber soles. How classy was I?

When my callback went well, I was asked to come in again the next day. This put a small wrinkle in our plan since my brother and I only had the clothes on our backs and a bunch of dead batteries, and by the way, we needed to get back to Port Authority by four p.m. or we would miss our connecting bus in Boston. Naturally, we told them it would be no problem and we were looking forward to coming in again the next day! My parents had given us about forty dollars, so they faxed a copy of their credit card to a squalid hotel and convinced the hotel manager that although their children were checking in now, they themselves would *of course* be along later that day; what kind of children would be staying in a hotel room in New York City alone?

The next morning, against our parents' explicit orders, we went out in search of the Village—specifically, Bleecker and MacDougal. Our dad had talked about that corner with affection and awe, and we could see why. Each corner of the intersection had a café that looked like something we'd only seen in movies. My dad probably meant, like, the music scene in the sixties, but we shared a plate of pancakes and figured life would never get better than this. None of those cafés are there anymore, and I don't want to sound like one of those people who complains, "Oh, New York has changed so much, it isn't what it used to be," except that that's a LIE. I have ALWAYS wanted to be one of those people, and now I am!

After our adventure, we went to my second callback. I could tell it was going well, because they were keeping me in the room for a long time. This is the only metric I have; I black out in auditions, even to this day. As my brother and I left, an assistant jogged after us. She caught up to us at the elevator and said, "You're doing great, and we want to bring you back again tomorrow"—she swallowed and lowered her voice—"but we were wondering if you had anything else to wear? Maybe we could see you in some nicer shoes or something?"

Instead of saying, "No, bitch, I came down here on a bus and

I washed my socks and underwear in a hotel sink this morning," we assured her that we were all over it, no problem, message received. I had no idea what they were looking for, but I knew that no matter what a casting director said, you were supposed to agree and figure it out later. It was dark out when we left the casting office, so we decided to wake up early the next day to buy me some respectable shoes with what was left of our cash.

The next morning we asked the receptionist at the hotel where to find the nearest Payless. At this point in our program, I'd like to gently remind anyone who thought that was a punch line to check yourself. Finding respectable shoes for girls at Payless is perfectly normal for lots of families. I mention it by name in this story because it makes me feel sentimental, not because it's supposed to be ironic. To the people reading this thinking, *We already knew it was normal, don't be so preachy*, I apologize; I have been around rich people too long and it has made me defensive.

It took almost all morning and into the afternoon to find a pair of shoes that looked dressy but left us with enough cash to get McDonald's before we caught the bus home. Eventually, we found a pair of white strappy sandals that were a size too big, but they were on sale, so they were coming with me! I slipped them on with my wide-leg jeans and my ratty sweater and thought, *I've done it! I look like a rich girl!* I still looked like a delinquent who didn't know how to brush her hair, but now I had white shoes.

I went to my final audition. I blacked out. We caught the bus home.

My brother and I kept repeating that I shouldn't get too excited. I shouldn't count my chickens. I was twelve, but I'd experienced enough rejection that I had a system in place for managing my expectations. Somewhere around Hartford, we turned on the "for emergencies" phone. I had a voice mail saying I got the job. We celebrated for however long it takes a busload of people to wake up and scream at you.

jaded old chorus girl

I lost a Tony Award to Broadway legend Audra McDonald when I was twelve, so I've been a bitter bitch since before my first period. I'm very proud to have lost that Tony to Ms. McDonald. She is one of the finest talents in the theater world and genuine Broadway royalty. I also feel that if I had *won* and made a televised speech at age twelve, the delayed embarrassment would have been so severe, I'd currently be a Howard Hughes–style shut-in, but without the money for the mansion or the planes or the legion of servants to take away bottles of my urine.

Starting in theater gave me a basic work ethic that I may not have gotten if I started in film and television. I worked six days a week, eight shows a week (two shows on Wednesdays and Saturdays, Mondays off). It wasn't so much the schedule—I worked in accordance with child labor laws—it was that I was held accountable for my work.

Once, during rehearsals, our director was playing with the shape of a musical number that involved most of the cast— which jokes should stay, where they should go, etc. He decided to try reinstituting a small joke I'd had in a previous draft, and we started the number again from the top. I lost where we were in the music and I opened my mouth to say the line, a measure too late. He was already shaking his head and signaling the pianist to stop.

"Anna just lost a line. Let's go back to how it was before and start again."

Okay. Those are the rules and I will operate within them from now on. I'll just double my memorization efforts, pretend I'm not crying, and see you all again tomorrow! Beyond tutoring breaks every three hours, I didn't get special treatment.

When I booked *High Society*, it was unclear how long I would be in New York. My contract was for six months, but shows can go under after a few weeks of poor ticket sales. Since my dad was a substitute teacher at the time, he was able to move to New York with me, and my mother stayed in Maine with my brother.

We rented an apartment in Yonkers ("we" is accurate; he signed the rental agreement, but I was the one who paid for it) and commuted into the city each day. Yonkers was not very glamorous, but it was cheaper and I was being paid the union minimum. When you are from Maine and you get a job on Broadway, you take what they offer. Between my accountant mother and my former-banker father, I'm sure a budget was worked out, but by the time the show was in tech rehearsals, it was clear to my dad that it was not manageable.

I have no idea if Dad had been planning to say something, but one day when he was dropping me off at rehearsals, the producer walked past us and casually asked, "How are things, Will?"

"Well, Michael, not good." My dad is plainspoken. It's a

wonderful quality that I feel lucky to have inherited and that has gotten me in trouble more times than I can count.

"When my daughter is grown, she can make the decision to starve for her art. She can live in a one-bedroom apartment with five people and work a second job during the day, but we aren't going to be able to make this work any longer, and I'm going to take her home unless we figure something out."

The ultimate negotiation tactic? Be willing to walk away. I certainly wasn't willing, but my dad was, and as he said, I wasn't grown and it wasn't my decision.

The producers agreed to give me a weekly per diem, and that kept us afloat while we were in New York. (When the show closed I had nothing left over, but I won the final "five-dollar Friday" draw and went home with around $250 in cash. Each bill had the name of a cast or crew member written on it, and I cherished them. I vowed never to spend them. When I got to high school, I started dipping into my stash to chip in whenever someone's older sister would buy us booze until all the bills were gone. I know. It's all so *Little Girl Lost*.)

It wasn't a financial win, but the experience was incredible. The show was based on the movie musical *High Society* with Grace Kelly, which was based on the movie (and stage play) *The Philadelphia Story* with Katharine Hepburn. The plot centers on a woman who is about to marry the wrong man and the complications that arise the weekend before her wedding. I played the woman's little sister. I had a bunch of solid lines, a funny musical number, and a great piece of physical comedy in the second act that only once drew blood mid-performance.

The cast and crew were sweet beyond words. They were en-
couraging and serious and they believed in me. They told me
to stay focused on dance lessons, despite my apparent lack of
aptitude; held half-serious competitions for crying on cue; and
recommended movies and books that they felt "smart young
women" should know. Lisa Banes, who played my mother, would
lightly bounce along to the music before our entrance and whisper in an old-timey voice, "Let's go do a great big Broadway
show." How great is that?!

They treated me like I was family and wanted to make sure
that my real family was okay under the stress of one parent moving to New York. Once a month my dad and I would drive home

to Maine after the Sunday matinee and make it back in time for the Tuesday night show. On those days the entire cast would speed up their dialogue and cut off every laugh a moment too soon so that I could beat traffic. Only one cast member indulged in languid pauses during those performances, and our conductor, Paul Gemignani, would punish her by radically speeding up the tempo of her songs.

One of my closest friends asked me recently if I had a favorite memory from my career. I do, but it's not my own. It's one of those stories I was told so often that I can picture it as clearly as if I were there. The only reason I'm certain I wasn't is because I was onstage at the time.

The first time my mom came to visit, my dad snuck her into the alley just outside the stage door and told her to listen.

"They're almost done. That's the curtain call music." He leaned in a little closer to the door and held up a finger. They listened quietly. Suddenly the applause swelled.

"That's for her."

My mom burst into tears.

I love this story. Luckily, most of the stuff that made my mom proud didn't revolve around me performing.

I hit the jackpot. I didn't have to go to school (my dad was tutoring me) and I got to run around New York City all day. Sometimes I was lonely. I met most of the other kids who were in shows at the time, but as I said, child actors are crazy, and the conversations often looked like this:

"Anna Kendrick is a great name. Is that a stage name or your real name?"

"It's my real name."

"You got a good one. Good syllabic symmetry."

I'd try to catch my dad's eye and find some recognition that this was not normal preadolescent behavior.

I did make a few friends. My closest friend was Nora, an understudy in *The Sound of Music*. *The Sound of Music* kids were intimidating. They seemed like this sexy, co-ed gang (proving once again that even the dorkiest subcultures have their rock stars). Nora was the only thing I had that resembled normal preteen life. We had sleepovers and went window shopping, we sang along to pop music and show tunes, and each of us tried to convince the other that *she* was the pretty one.

Even though I was friends with Nora, we didn't see each other all the time, and I had no other good friends. Sometimes working and commuting didn't feel as easy as it did other days. I knew the show like the back of my hand, but I still had to do it every night.

Sometimes I would get home after a show and I couldn't sleep. I'd sneak into the living room and watch TV until the sun came up. Then I'd sleep all day and dread going to work. I'd dread the drive from Yonkers. I'd dread putting on my costume. I'd dread warming up. I'd dread my entrance. I'd dread my first line. I'd dread my song. I'd dread the drive home.

I was so happy to be doing this incredible thing, but at this point, dear reader, I'd like to use my one "What do you want from me, I was twelve years old, tired and lonely and working the kind of job that full-grown adults do" card.

I needed a break. Just a little one. Anxiety typically only becomes unmanageable for me when I feel I have no choice, when

I feel trapped. I just needed a break in routine so I could shake out the dread.

One day, when we were halfway through the first act, I reached my limit. I needed to take a break RIGHT NOW. Don't get too excited; this isn't a story about me bailing on a Broadway show mid-performance. I told my dad that I didn't want to do the show the next night. He knew I wouldn't be asking if I wasn't serious and kind of desperate. At intermission, we went to speak to the stage manager . . . no, it was a producer, maybe . . . I remember we were under the stage, but who the hell was in charge of that? Who did you talk to about taking a night off and why the hell was their office under the stage?* At any rate, my dad told the appropriate woman that I was going to stay home and rest the following night.

"Well, tomorrow night is tough." She winced. "It would be a lot easier for everyone if you took off a night next week."

Just being near a serious conversation between adults made my stomach turn (it still does, actually), and when she looked over at me she could see that I was upset.

"Do you want a glass of water, honey?"

In show business, when you tell people that you need something and it runs counter to what they want from you, it's amazing how often they will offer you water. This is code for *Deal with it.*

I agreed that having a night off the following week would be just as good. The advance notice *would* make it less stressful for my coworkers, and I really didn't want anyone to be mad at me.

---

* My memory is bad and I could probably ask myself these kinds of questions on every page, but I'm going to do my best to fill in the blanks from here on out, and I hope you're cool with that, too. XO!

We scheduled my night off for a Tuesday so that, coupled with the Monday (which was always off), I would have a real weekend of sorts. My dad took me up to the Catskills. We went to a mall, and I swam in the hotel pool, and I even rode a fat, probably dying horse at a nearby ranch.

In the car on the ride home, I was quiet, and Dad said, "You really needed the night off when you said you did, huh?"

I nodded and he hit the steering wheel. I hated that he was mad. Which is weird since he was only mad because he hadn't been able to make me happy. Love is some funny shit, right?

When the show closed, I was sad but relieved. I was ready to go home. Still, maybe because I'd seen my family struggle to pay the bills, even while my father was working two jobs, it was disconcerting to be unemployed. Sure, I could go home and go to school and see my friends and family, but at what cost? Was I a twelve-year-old has-been?

I'm still haunted by this fear. It has made me very cautious of feeling comfortable in my career—and turned me into a bit of a workaholic.

Even now, every job I get, I worry that it will be my last. I think becoming a washed-up hag is sort of my destiny. So if you see a wrinkled old bitch wearing a tattered fur and chain-smoking in an off-Broadway back alley . . . that's just me. Starting four years from now.

hell, thy name is middle school

In elementary school, we had an afternoon of "health class" once a year. The teachers separated us by gender and explained what we could expect from puberty. They handed out maxi pads to the girls and gave the boys . . . pamphlets on styling a wispy mustache that ONLY grows at the corners of your mouth? I may never know.

There was a lot of emphasis on how excited we should be to start our periods. This is a dirty trick, but now I understand why it's necessary. It comes for us all, so there's no point working little girls into a panic over it. However, there was perhaps *too* much emphasis on the *magic* of becoming a woman. So much so that I missed a few key points on the logistics of menstruation. For example, I thought that once you got your period you had it every day, all the time, for the rest of your life. This sounded pretty awful, but the girls on the tampon boxes looked excited about it, and I trusted anyone who could rock a side ponytail.

I was also promised an "awkward" stretch of time when all the girls would tower over the boys. For me, that moment would never come. In middle school, hiding the fact that I still shopped in the kids' section became almost a full-time job.

In elementary school, being the smallest was cute. It had given me an identity, even made me feel special. But you know how thirteen-year-olds don't want to hang out with eight-year-olds? They don't want to hang out with you if you *look* eight years old, either.

My height made me an easy mark. When my sixth-grade crush enumerated the reasons he wouldn't date any of the girls in our class, my label was "too short." I laughed, then retired to the girls' bathroom, where I got on my knees and prayed to Jesus to make me taller. No one in the world was suffering more than me.

Once girls started getting boobs, a whole new area of un-creative slams emerged. "Hey, Anna, you should date a pirate, because they love sunken chests." Where do boys learn these insults? Is there a manual? Is *that* what they got in health class?!

When I came back from doing *High Society*, no one my age cared. (Despite *High Society* being the eighteenth-longest-running Broadway show ever!*) I had hoped my classmates might be impressed, but weirdly, a picture of me in the local paper singing in pigtails did not make me the hit of the school.

While no one at Lincoln Junior High especially cared about my New York sabbatical, dance and music classes gave me a level playing field of equally dorky contemporaries to befriend. I even went to overnight choir camp in the summer. (I'll say that again in case you weren't already in love with me . . . *choir camp.*) It was the only place where I was the cool girl. Well, not

---

* That year.

Man-eater.

cool maybe, but I stood a chance. It's no surprise then that in my professional career I have played a "cool girl" character precisely once, in *Pitch Perfect*, a movie about choir.

In eighth grade my crush was the new kid, Darryl. He'd transferred from somewhere exotic that I remember being New York or Chicago but was probably Canada. On his first day, a girl in gym class got hit hard with a basketball and dropped to the ground, holding her head. We all stood there with our mouths open, but Darryl scooped her up like it was nothing and carried her to the nurse's office. The kid ran heroically to her aid! Like an adult in a movie! Why couldn't that head injury have been mine?!

One day a girl asked me—in front of Darryl—what size my pants were. Middle school was a time when kids asked each other all kinds of inappropriate questions, and if you didn't answer, *you* were the weird one. She was trying to expose me as a genetic freak, still forced to shop at the Limited Too because of my undersized arms, legs, and everything else. Guess what, haters, I'd been shopping that very weekend! (Jesus, take the wheel!) I'd been to Wet Seal—which was trashy, but at least it wasn't a store for children—and found a pair of jeans that I didn't have to pin in the back.

I shrugged and said, "A small, I guess?"

"Don't you mean a children's size twelve?" She turned to Darryl. "She still shops at, like, Gap Kids." (I didn't. Gap Kids was too expensive.)

Oh, you stupid bitch.

"No, they're from Wet Seal," I said, pulling out the tag to prove their origin. "Yeah, it's a zero, I guess."

"It's a double zero," she pointed out, still trying to shame me. Today I assume she passes her time flaying old ladies for sport.

In a flash, I realized I could say, "So? Are girls not supposed to have small waists?"

"No, no," Darryl said, "that's proper."

I had abruptly crossed over into the land where being small was a good thing! And Darryl had spoken four words to me! Suck it, you crone!!

It should be noted that a double zero was a good fit for a

thirteen-year-old girl who was so painfully underdeveloped she didn't get her period for another three years. If you *aren't* a size double zero, congratulations, you don't look ten anymore.

That was the best interaction I'd ever had with Darryl. I figured I'd take that little seedling and let it blossom; hit my stride once we got to high school, and I (fingers crossed) got boobs. I'd play the long game. Alas, he moved away again after eighth grade. And I did not get boobs in time for high school.

Yet looking young—a source of crippling insecurity—was a huge professional asset. My agent was thrilled I wasn't growing. As long as you still look the part, casting directors value a few extra years of experience and maturity. Plus, child labor laws are more relaxed. Couldn't the kids at school see this was good for my career?

A lot of the kids I'd met in New York were taking breaks to "just be a kid" for a while. Were they crazy?? I wanted to "just be a kid" as much as the next guy, but I wasn't about to take a career in the arts for granted. There are only a handful of parts for children on Broadway at any given time, and maybe the paucity of roles should have been a sign that taking a break wouldn't hurt. But I could see a future where I got drunk at office parties and babbled about how I'd been a child star (because my alternate-reality self would definitely overstate her former glory).

The first thing I booked after *High Society* was the musical version of *Jane Eyre*. It was in the workshop phase, when the producers assemble a cast to run through a show for a couple of weeks. The idea is to get the show on its feet so that it can be improved before a potential Broadway run. Based on each workshop, the writer, composer, and director will go away and make changes, then do it all again. Sometimes all the actors are re-hired. Sometimes they aren't.

There was a challenging but thrilling piece of music for Young Jane that had made the role difficult to cast. Consequently, I was treated like a bit of a unicorn. The producers sent up prayers (in direct opposition to my bathroom-stall plea) that I would stay the same size. But the show was at least a year away from get-ting to Broadway. Occasionally, I'd catch the producers tilting their heads at me, gauging my height with an invisible yardstick. I made a point to transition my rehearsal attire from chunky boots to thin-soled ballet flats and ruefully dug out my Limited Too best to look as young as possible.

I was with that show for about a year, doing additional work-shops or giving special cabaret-style performances to rooms of potential investors. But after a while, a bittersweet atmosphere took hold. There was a consolatory vibe at what would be my last performance, but I didn't know why. I would have recog-nized the behavior if I'd ever had a boyfriend: I was about to get dumped.

I was sad to lose the job. My disappointment was slightly allayed when I heard they'd had to cut Young Jane's song be-cause they couldn't find a replacement to sing it. That might not have been true; the song slowed down the pacing of the first act anyway.

This was not the only time I would lose a job this way, but I confess I was grateful for every inch I gained. Finding even one article of adult clothing that fit me seemed like a reasonable trade-off to being fired. Maybe I should have prioritized my professional pursuits, but my home life always felt equally significant. Decorating my locker seemed just as important as getting new headshots.

I had to compartmentalize, because everyone else did. People at school didn't care that I had an audition for *Touched by an Angel,* and, weirdly, casting directors didn't care that I had a four-page French assignment or that Courtney from choir was being mean to me for NO REASON.

While I was in one place, I tried not to think about the other. It was sort of like living a double life. Like a *spy*! Yeah. I was like James Bond. Like a loud, unsexy James Bond.

MGM, the next time you want to reboot the franchise, you know where to find me.

camp

The summer before my senior year of high school, I went to New York and made a nonunion film called *Camp*. It was a unique film in many ways. People have either never heard of it or they want to tell me that it changed their life, no matter how inappropriate the circumstances. I am very glad this movie helped you come out to your parents, and as I was saying, my insurance only covers the generic form of RectaGel.

Camp was written and directed by Todd Graff, based on his real experiences at Stagedoor Manor, the (in)famous children's theater camp in upstate New York. Stagedoor is a haven for every young misfit out there who'd just die if they were forced to be in one more school-sanctioned production of *Peter Pan*. The camp is known for putting on arguably inappropriate shows with its young campers. Imagine *The Glass Menagerie* or *Once on This Island*—a musical about tensions between the light- and dark-skinned Haitians—with an all-white preteen cast. It's not universally relatable material for a movie.

Because the movie was replete with song and dance, a month-long rehearsal period was scheduled in Manhattan. Most of the cast members were local, but some of us had nowhere to stay for the duration of rehearsals, so indie production company Killer Films found competitively priced living spaces to accommodate their out-of-town actors. For example, I lived in the walk-in pantry of a small uptown apartment shared by three film students. Don't worry, the film students were really nice and the pantry was mostly empty.

I had no complaints. It was summer, I was sixteen, I got to take the subway to work in the morning and learn music and choreography all day. I was going to internet cafés to check my email, the film students were explaining things like "establishing shots"* and "coverage"† to me, and I was on my own. Sure, I wasn't really a New York resident, and I wasn't getting paid, but I felt like such a grown-up. *Wait 'til the kids at choir camp hear what I did this summer.*

Toward the end of the rehearsal period, our choreographer, Broadway legend Jerry Mitchell, stopped us for a pep talk. We were exhausted and he was about to tell us to get our shit together. He said that whether we liked it or not, this movie was going to be around forever and that what we put on film in the coming months would, unlike theater, exist long after we were dead. It was super dark and probably should have scared me off making movies forever.

---

* The first shot of a new scene that establishes the location for the audience. You know how on *Seinfeld* there's always a shot of the exterior of the diner before they cut inside and we see the gang slowly ruining their lives? That's the establishing shot!

† After the first wide "master shot" of a scene is done, the subsequent camera angles (close-ups, two-shots, etc.) are considered coverage. You know the opening sequence of *Boogie Nights*? It's the opposite of that.

What can I say? I was living in a pantry, I was getting yelled at in dance rehearsal—if I wasn't living the dream, I don't know who was.

Weirdly, my excitement did not stem from the fact that I was about to be in my first film. I guess, if I'm honest, it didn't feel like we were making a real movie. Real movies had famous actors in them, like Tom Hanks or the German lady from *Austin Powers* (my metric was all over the place). And films about teenagers had gorgeous, polished, twenty-five-year-old actors, and the plots revolved around summer crushes—not going to prom in drag and getting your ass kicked.

I don't mean to suggest that I didn't believe in what we were doing, I just couldn't imagine a world where anyone outside the cast was ever going to see it. I knew that tiny films like *Clerks* or *The Blair Witch Project* could be huge, but I wasn't sure that musical numbers from Burt Bacharach's *Promises, Promises* or jokes about Stephen Sondheim were going to play wide. I also knew that Killer Films had made dark, important films like *Kids* and *Boys Don't Cry*, but again, *Promises, Promises* and Stephen Sondheim.

My big problem was Fritzi, a weird girl with greasy hair and terrible clothes who happened to be the character I was playing. Fritzi was the camp loser and she was obsessed with (and probably in love with) Jill, the hot, popular girl at camp.

Today, I would be thrilled to play such a twisted little character. At the time, I just wanted to wear makeup and have my hair done, like the other girls in the cast. I wanted to downplay the ambiguously sexual nature of Fritzi's (very much unrequited) interest in Jill. I wanted to be likable onscreen. I still had to go back to high school once this was over, and I so badly wanted to be the hot girl in a movie, not the girl who washes the hot girl's underwear by hand.

A few years ago, Diane Lane gave an interview where she admitted that she was equally conflicted about one of her first film roles. She played the talentless front woman of a rock band in (the wonderful) *Ladies and Gentlemen, the Fabulous Stains*, and she hated that the band was supposed to be terrible. She wanted to be an onscreen rock star. I hear that, sister. Sixteen-year-old insecurity is a real impediment to truth in art.

The very first scene on our very first day was a long and complicated tracking shot on the street near the West Side Highway that involved almost the whole cast. After each take, we'd just stare at each other, waiting to hear if we needed to do it again. I didn't know it then, but that's sort of how it always feels. I heard Todd laugh that the people at Killer Films were going to be pissed when they saw the footage, because there was no coverage (I knew what that meant!).

That first scene was the only thing we shot in Manhattan, and when we finished, we piled into vans and drove up to a vacant camp in the Catskills, the real Stagedoor Manor, where we would shoot the rest of the film. In interviews, lots of actors say that making a movie is "like sleepaway camp." They have no idea.

There was no phone, no TV, no internet, and no cell reception. If you weren't working on a certain day (or a certain week), too bad. No one had a car, so you weren't leaving. We got paid seventy-five dollars a day on the days we worked, and only on the days we worked. This is why unions matter.

The blessing was that the other cast members were wonderful. Without the aid of cell phones, we spent our days off wandering around the camp to see who else wanted to hang out. It was as close as I ever got to having a gang of neighborhood friends, like I'd seen in movies from the nineties about growing up in the seventies. Our ages ranged from twelve to twenty-five and our interests ranged from musical theater to music. Or theater.

We found a few board games in the main offices but got sick of them quickly and spent most of our time engaging in general nerdery. We held *Waiting for Guffman* trivia competitions and took makeshift dance classes from a cast member who had obsessively collected bootleg videos of Twyla Tharp shows. Sasha and Tiffany, the two best singers, taught each other riffs and tested them out in parallel harmony while the rest of us listened in disbelief. Casual singing became so normalized that when I went home, it took me weeks to stop peppering my conversations with melodic interludes.

I shot my first real scene about a week into our stay. That morning, I got into my awful wardrobe, a woman rubbed down my frizzy hair with fistfuls of men's pomade, and I went to the set (a.k.a. I walked three minutes to a different part of the camp).

We did a few final rehearsals in the set of "Jill's" bedroom, and Todd told us we were going to film the next one. Someone yelled "last looks," which meant that three people came into the room and poked at me: the wardrobe department pulled my sleeves back down to my wrists, the hair department gave me another handful of grease, and the makeup department looked me over to make sure I hadn't secretly applied lip gloss again, like I'd done the first day.

This new ritual of last-minute touch-ups taught me that actors could become unfilmably ugly at any moment and needed to be beautified at ten-minute intervals. At first, it felt like pampering, but very quickly it became the standard by which I measured how insecure I should feel that day.

The scene was really just a conversation between Fritzi, my character, and Jill, the object of her obsession. It was creepy content, but pretty straightforward in terms of filmmaking. Back on the first day in the city, we had filmed the whole scene at once, in an open space, with complicated blocking. It had felt like a piece of theater. This was just two people in a room talking at each other.

Once Jill had been glossed, fluffed, and shimmered and I'd been, well . . . greased, we stood on our start marks and waited for "Action." We did the scene, just like we'd done it in rehearsals, and eventually heard Todd's voice call "Cut" from the next room.

That was it; that was my first time filming a scene in a movie. It might have driven me to distraction had it not been so . . . ordinary. I'd only ever performed in front of an audience before. The audience was a barometer of your success or failure. The audience gave you energy; their presence filled the room with a kind of electricity that told you, *This is it, this is happening!* The "audience" on a film set was just your director and the perpetually bored crew. Filming a movie felt exactly like *not* filming a movie.

I've come to love film sets and see the low-key environment as an asset, but it's still unnerving that you can finish a scene and not know how it went. Things that crack you up while you're filming can go over like a lead balloon in the movie, and things that feel stilted and boring on set can be tense and exciting for a viewer. While you're shooting, you rely on the director to tell you if it's going well, and you have to trust that they're right. With my favorite directors, at least four times per shoot I'll think, *That is a fucking terrible idea, let's do it.*

I went back to my room and wondered what we'd done. I couldn't ask anyone for advice because none of us had ever been in a movie before. My next scene involved six actors and was my first lesson in what it feels like when a scene is *not* going well.

The scene had a fair bit of exposition, a few jokes, and some good old-fashioned bitchy teen drama. In a practical sense, though, it had six first-time film actors slogging their way through two pages of dialogue.

Everyone was making a meal out of their bits, fumbling punch lines, adding overdramatic inflection to minor lines. Todd was getting frustrated. At one point I heard him say, "I forgot that I'm not working with actors." He didn't mean it as a dig—we were just making mistakes that experienced film actors would not. I thought, *Yeah, guys, come on, we don't need to take these long pauses before every little line*. I then proceeded to take a long pause before my one line.

Once I recognized that I was a total hypocrite, I started jumping in at warp speed in every subsequent take. It was a little weird, but it was an improvement.

Shooting the musical numbers helped bridge the gap between theater and film. We shot them in the various tiny theaters at the camp and performed them exactly like we would have onstage. Okay, this we knew how to do. We happily did them over and over as the cameras were repositioned around the theater.

Fritzi's solo number was "The Ladies Who Lunch" from the musical *Company*. It's a wildly inappropriate song for a teenage girl and was even more bizarre coming from one with the body of a twelve-year-old. This peculiar situation arises in the film because Fritzi has poisoned Jill after being rejected by her and steals the role mid-performance. She then sings a song about the ennui of middle-aged womanhood and her disillusionment with the bourgeoisie who surround her privileged 1970s Manhattan life. Sure.

When we finished shooting the number, we were supposed

to get a shot of Jill watching me from backstage, furious and still throwing up, but Todd said he was going to scrap it. He whispered to me, "You don't cut away from lightning in a bottle." I'd never heard the expression before—in fact, for years I thought it was his personal invention—but I knew it meant I'd done well. He was the whole audience, so I had to trust him.

My mom came to pick me up on the last day of filming. I wept so hard and for so long that she pulled the car over, thinking I was going to need medical attention.

I haven't cried at the wrap of a film since. At the time, I couldn't reconcile the fact that no matter what we told each other, I would never go back there, never be with those people ever again. Now, I see catch-and-release as part of the beauty of what I get to do. Then again, I haven't been stuck on a campground with twenty people and no technology for two months since, so maybe it was just the only time I've experienced Stockholm syndrome.

After filming wrapped, I went back to Maine and started the school year. Each time I described it to friends it felt less and less real. There were no famous actors in it. The plot sounded ludicrous. I had no point of reference to give. If *High School Musical* had already been made I could have described it as "like *High School Musical*, but with songs you'll probably hate." I kept my expectations low.

Six months later, I found out the movie had been selected for the Sundance Film Festival. I was over the moon. I couldn't wait to tell people. But I held off—I had to find the right time to announce that the coolest thing that could possibly happen was happening.

Before winter vacation our French teacher had us go around the room and say what we were doing over the break "*en Français, s'il vous plait.*" Well, thank you very much, Madame Cadot, for this perfect opportunity. I reported my news. No one in the room even blinked. This was French Six. These motherfuckers understood me. Did they really not know what I was talking about? Maine is small, but we're not devoid of culture. What the hell? Why are you not impressed with me?!

Killer Films booked three hotel rooms at the festival, meant for the three lead actors only, but everyone else in the movie flew themselves out with the unspoken understanding that we'd all be crashing with them. Three to a bed, everyone else on the floor. It was glorious.

We were gleefully aware of our status as the ragtag nonunion group in a sea of real, SAG card–carrying actors. We went to gifting suites that refused to give us anything, reveled in the bright cold, holding fancy coffees we had no intention of drinking, and took advantage of the parties by sending one of our legal cast members to the open bar for seven drinks at a time.

I saw Oliver Platt going into his hotel and executed my first—and last—celebrity approach.

"Oh my god, you're Oliver Platt! I loved you so much in *Dangerous Beauty*!"

He smiled and thanked me. I smiled expectantly at him for too long and eventually he told me to have a nice afternoon and went on his way. It was a strange interaction, and I left it feeling dissatisfied but not knowing what I'd hoped would happen. I'm terrible in every social situation; I don't know why I thought it would go *better* with a famous person. I vowed to never approach a celebrity again.

On our second day at the festival, we shuffled into reserved seats at the back of the Library Theatre to watch our movie. The film screened and something surreal happened. It played HUGE. People were laughing. A lot. They got all the in-jokes about *Who's Afraid of Virginia Woolf?* and *'Night, Mother* and *Stella Dallas*. I didn't even get the joke about *Stella Dallas*.

When subservient Fritzi poisons Jill, Todd tapped me on the shoulder and whispered, "Get ready." Fritzi deadpans, "The goddamn show must go on," and the theater exploded in cheers. I felt electrified. I was just sitting in the audience, but my ears were ringing like I'd been struck by lightning.

When the credits rolled, each character's face appeared for a moment, with the actor's name at the bottom of the screen. I gripped my seat waiting for mine. My face came up, and again, that electric feeling went through me. It was MY name. I'm not sure I can explain this properly, but I was still expecting to see my character's name. This was MY name. This was the name my mother called me and my teachers called me and the neighborhood kid who flashed his penis at me in fifth grade had called me. Seeing it on film gave me the same feeling you get when you see yourself in the background of a photo you didn't know was being taken. I didn't feel especially proud or accomplished—if anything, it reminded me what a dummy I was for being so surprised to be listed under my own name—but seriously, guys, holy shit.

Then the strangest thing happened. The audience was on its feet. For a movie with no real actors in it. For a movie about losers who sang show tunes. For a movie that looked like crap and had no production value.

We went out and partied like only a group of dorky teens and young adults who've just had an incredible first screening of their weird movie could. That is to say, we crashed the *Pieces of April* party and drank them out of house and home.

Trying to blend in with the established Sundance crowd and succeeding.

The next day, I got a call from a friend back home. At this point, Sundance was at the height of its unintentional rebranding from respected independent film festival to celebrity hangout. In fact, the following year, Paris Hilton showed up for no reason, which actually helped the backlash reach critical mass, and soon after, Sundance returned to being more about movies than celebrities. (Although I'm told it won't ever be the same as it was in the nineties. We get it, Kevin Smith; it was real back then.) My friend made small talk for a while, then said, "Hey, my mom was just watching *Access Hollywood* and it said something about Britney Spears and Fred Durst being at Sundance right now. Isn't that weird? You're at something called Sundance, and then THE Sundance, with the famous people, is going on at the same time. Did you know that?"

"What? No, I'm . . . what are you talking about? I am at THE Sundance."

"What do you mean?"

"I'm in a movie that is playing at the Sundance Film Festival right now."

"Wait, really? Have you seen Britney Spears?"

I had not seen Britney Spears, but this conversation recontextualized the underwhelming response I'd gotten in French class. They had heard of the Sundance Film Festival; they just thought I must have meant something else. I suppose it would be like a coworker you'd known for years telling you they were about to compete in the Olympic trials. You assume they meant, like, the company Olympics, and forget all about it.

"No, I haven't seen Britney Spears, but the movie got a standing ovation, which everyone says is really rare here. And I met Oliver Platt!"

"Oh. Ross called Lauren S. to ask if they had biology homework for winter break, but she says that she saw him write down the assignment in class."

"No! Did Jenna dump him?"

Double life. James Bond.

The movie came out and did not do well. The beauty and curse of Sundance is that the screenings are packed with film lovers, most of whom connect to the pain of being an outsider and get obscure references. They are also generous audiences for new talent. They forgave a lot of the film's flaws.

Marketing the movie to the general public as a teen romp backfired enormously, and many people who thought they were going to see a musical *American Pie* were turned off by the homosexuality, cross-dressing, and vintage synthesizers. They were also less forgiving of the uneven quality of a low-budget film.

Being in that theater at Sundance is one of the great memories of my career, and maybe my life, so far. But when I met a guy in London the following year who said the movie was boring and weird, I couldn't fault him. And when I met a girl six months ago who told me she named her car and her dog Fritzi, I made a mental note of her distinguishing features in case I had to describe her later for a police sketch.

the mayor of squaresville

I like to tell people that I'm a square. It's a charming way to warn someone that I'm a finicky little brat without freaking them out. I got to work with Lisa Kudrow recently, and when she told me she thought she was probably an even bigger square, I maintained that couldn't be true. We traded stories for a while, trying to out-straitlace each other.

For example, I told her about the time my friend found out I'd never seen a movie without paying and he forced me to sneak in to *Iron Man*. I did not enjoy the film at all; I felt guilty the entire time. And when I found myself at dinner with Jon Favreau and Robert Downey Jr. a year later, I confessed my crime and insisted on giving them cash or buying them something on the menu of commensurate value. Lisa knew she'd found an uptight, apple-polishing soul sister. We held a little election to see who would be the ruler of Squaresville, if such a miraculous place existed. I was elected mayor and she, my loyal deputy. To be fair, the thing was rigged in our favor since we were the only two people organized enough to bother voting.

I happen to love rules. I love having a plan. I love a film set that's run like a well-oiled machine. I thrive in structure; I drown in chaos. I love rules and I love following them. Unless that rule is stupid. And yes, I have felt qualified, no matter my age, to make that determination. Scrupulous people don't enjoy causing trouble, but they can be defiant as hell.

As an adult, being square is more or less an acceptable personality trait. The only time I desperately wanted to be rebellious was in adolescence. I wanted to be Rizzo, not Sandra Dee! I had to will myself to break rules when I could stomach it. While I'll admit I enjoyed the thrill, I was not "the bad kid." In fact, aside from the following stories, I was a painfully typical example of "the good kid." During free period, even on the rare Maine sunny day, I'd stay in the cafeteria and do my Latin homework. Not because I was smart, but because I assumed the fabric of the universe would disintegrate if I didn't. But the qualities that made me a square as a teenager—dedication, independence, maturity—led me to break the biggest rule of all. I committed systematic genocide. (Is she kidding? Let's read on and find out!)

My adolescent flirtations with rule-breaking were alternately facilitated and foiled by my brother, Mike. Mike was a genuine cool kid. Not a "popular" kid; a wiry, quick-witted, slightly dangerous, well-liked kid. He'd been bullied in middle school but at fifteen he shot past six feet, got into good music and minor drug use, and stalked around the school in baggy white tees and fitted baseball caps. He had that feral look about him that was specific to the early 2000s, like the actors in the movie *Kids* (a movie I should not have watched before puberty). Like me, he had a strict sense of justice, so he had no interest in being unkind or intimidating people who were perfectly harmless, but he once beat up a friend for trying crystal meth and promised it would happen again if he slipped up. He was like a sheriff or an angsty Robin Hood. He'd be the first to point out what a loser I was, but wouldn't let anyone else say a word against me. He once made a kid apologize to me after making a crack about my size. ("I didn't know you were Kendrick's sister.") When I got home, Mike asked, "Did Spencer apologize to you today?"

"Yeah, he did! And do you know what I said back?"

"Don't tell me, dude. I know it's gonna be something lame."

It was something lame, so I'll spare him the embarrassment of putting it in this book.

I got better grades than Mike, but only because, as every teacher said, he didn't "apply himself." He eschewed all extracurricular activities in favor of hanging out in a park downtown that a local paper described as being full of "undesirables." That wasn't a description of the unsavory types that my brother might find there, that was a description of my brother. He drove states away to go to raves, which he called "parties," because only your parents and alarmed-looking blond ladies from the news said "raves."

When people would call the house and ask "Is Kendrick there?" I'd act irritated and say, "There are four Kendricks here, you'll have to be more specific." I always knew who they meant.

I still idolized him. He still thought I was a liability at best and figured that dictating my social life was in everyone's best interest.

At thirteen, I was invited to drink for the first time. Mike tore tickets at a local movie theater, and he and the rest of the teenage staff stayed behind after hours one night to throw a party. They had beer, vodka, and coffee brandy, a sickly sweet liqueur that you mix with milk. It's a staple of the low-income New England alcoholic, so naturally I started there. I wandered around the empty cinema, discovering what a buzz felt like and hearing, "Hey, loser, you still good?" at five-minute intervals.

At fourteen, he let me smoke a bowl with him and his best friend, Evan, whom I'd known since childhood. We went to T.G.I. Friday's and in a haze I said, "Do you guys feel like we're in a movie?" They laughed at me.

"Yeah, dude, that's the kind of stupid shit you need to get out of your system while you're just in front of us. Rookie."

That same year he took me to my first party (that's "rave" for all the people out there as lame as me). It was fun and weird, and I liked trying to pick up the dance style—though I might not have if I'd known how stupid I looked. I kept going whenever he would invite me, but mostly for the bragging rights. Mike told me I wouldn't be allowed to take Ecstasy until I was sixteen, which was fine with me since I found navigating new environments hard enough when I was sober.

When I was fifteen, we went separately to a warehouse rave upstate. I was paying for entry when a large young woman burst through the doors of the main floor, out into the makeshift lobby. She was still about ten feet away when she pointed at me and said, "No. Go home," and walked back inside. The guy who'd been taking my money shrugged and started to hand it back to me. If you're confused, it's because I mentioned that I was fifteen and you pictured a fifteen-year-old. But at this point, I looked about twelve. There weren't official age limits for a party thrown in a warehouse—certainly fifteen was old enough—yet she'd decreed I was too young.

This would not stand. It had taken hours to get there, and, more important, it was embarrassing. I paced away from the venue, wondering what to do, and scanned the small crowd of sweaty youths who had come outside for air. I spotted a friend of Mike's. This wasn't hard; he knew everyone.

"Hey, Travis! Go find Mike! Tell him they won't let me in!"

Ten minutes later my brother was outside and dragging me by the arm across the main floor. He planted me in front of the party's organizer.

"Trish, this is my sister. She's fifteen. We good?"

Trish took another look at me. "The age limit is sixteen."

I'd never seen my brother's powers of persuasion falter before.

"No it isn't, dude. There's a ton of kids in here who are fifteen. I'll bet you some are younger."

"Yeah, but Mike, look at her. She looks like a baby. If she ODs at my party, imagine how her picture's gonna look in the paper. No one would ever rent a space to me again. Any fifteen-year-old that *is* in there at least had the decency to look like a degenerate."

It was weird, but I kind of got her logic.

"Well, you don't have to worry about that. She doesn't do drugs. I told her she can't try X until she's sixteen. Let her in."

In your face, lady, I thought. I'd just been described as a goody two-shoes who left her drug-related decisions to her older brother, but I walked into the place looking like the smuggest little twelve-year-old there ever was.

Outside of underage substance use, my only dalliance in teen rule-breaking was some light shoplifting. Jesus, it's so trashy. It makes me cringe when I think of it.

I visited a friend in New York the summer I turned fourteen and she taught me. Oh, the city kids corrupting us weak-willed country folk! She also tried teaching me to flirt with guys, but soon found that was asking too much. Basically the trick to shoplifting was you went into a store, saw what you wanted, and took it without paying. Cute trick, right? Truthfully, the only thing she "showed" me was that it could be done. I think I would have gone my whole life without it occurring to me that normal people could just steal things. Pray I never witness a murder.

The small mercy was that this phase was short-lived. I got a friend in my hometown to shoplift with me (you know, pay it forward and all that) and for a while no Claire's or T.J. Maxx was safe. But, like a dying star, the desire burned brightly and disappeared quickly. A few years later I told my mother that I'd gone through a short thievery phase, and she was more surprised than angry. I suppose the statute of limitations for parental disapproval had passed.

That weekend, as we wheeled our groceries out of the Hannaford, she realized we'd forgotten cereal. We went back in and I grabbed it while she started looking for the shortest checkout line.

"Hey, Ma," I whispered, "you want me to just take it?"

I cocked my head down and opened my winter coat. She looked scandalized but kind of impressed, like I had a superpower, or we were on a date and I was the town bad boy. I put the cereal in the cart, but I swear, if I'd been serious she would have let me do it. Weak-willed country folk.

I remained a square, though. I had gone through the motions of a bare-minimum teenage rebellion, but it was all very Olivia Newton-John learning to blow smoke rings. It was just a prelude to breaking the biggest rule of all.

I started applying to colleges at the beginning of senior year. But I had this itch. I'd just come back from making *Camp*, and I already had more high school credits than I needed, which made going to class feel like I was in a holding pattern. I happen to love learning, but clawing through layers of disruptive students, overstretched teachers, and pointless extracurriculars to do it was discouraging. Deep down I knew I didn't want to go to college.

The idea of another four years of being chaperoned and dealing with immature classmates and putting off my real life made my chest tighten. But how could I not go?! Everyone in my family went to college; even my finally-got-his-act-together brother was in college. The value of education was ingrained in me from birth. In fact, I had thought college was mandatory until I was, like, thirteen and saw a commercial for the army. "I tried college; it wasn't for me," said the soldier. *"Wasn't for you"? What are you talking about? That's like saying that paying your taxes "wasn't for you"!* It turns out that was not correct, yet once I'd learned college was optional, I knew the suburban gossip would be that the Kendrick girl wasn't going because she was knocked up or criminally insane.

The itch was not going away, and even though I sent out my applications, I jumped at the first opportunity to put college on hold and start paying my dues. Fuck convention. Sandra Dee was going to the Big Apple.

LEAVING THE NEST

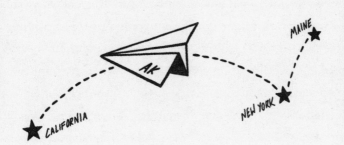

a little night music

I graduated high school early so that I could move to Manhattan and do *A Little Night Music* at New York City Opera, which is the braggiest sentence I will ever get to say. During this time, puberty finally hit me full force, which led to a number of horrifying incidents, including nearly passing out onstage because of the chest binder I had to wear to hide my new boobs.

Renting an apartment on my own and going to work at Lincoln Center made me feel *very* grown-up. I was constantly congratulating myself for the smallest things. *Yeah, I'm just riding the subway to work in New York City like it's no big deal.* Which of course meant that to me, at every moment, it was a HUGE deal. I wish I could say this masquerading-as-an-adult-and-getting-away-with-it feeling was exclusive to being seventeen, but so many things in my life are still like that. *Yeah, I'm checking my email on a laptop I own like it's no big deal.*

Night Music was the first real job I'd had since I was a kid, and I was desperate to do well. Also, Paul Gemignani, the musical director on *High Society* (who used to speed up that indulgent actress's songs), had recommended me for the role, and I didn't want to let him down. The cast was packed with impressive talents. My onstage grandmother and most frequent scene partner was played by none other than Claire Bloom, arguably the greatest living theater actress. Before I did the show, my dad found a VHS called *Shakespeare's Women & Claire Bloom*, which was half documentary, half master class. Watching it raised her to a godlike level in my eyes.

Working with someone with that kind of technique was beyond intimidating. I wish I could say that I shouldn't have been nervous, but the woman did not mince words. During our first attempt to rehearse our most intimate scene in the show, Claire stopped me mid-sentence and said, "You're not going to do it like that, are you?"

Well, Claire, I thought, *this was my audition scene, and that was how I did it in the audition . . . which got me this job. . . . So yeah, I thought I might.* I never forgave the director for not defending me. Together they decided what changes I should make. The net result was that I had to do almost the entire scene in profile, facing her.

If she saw me outside the rehearsal room, she would ask to run our scenes over and over. She once snapped her fingers while I was mid-line and said, "No, *really* do it; let's start again."

As we got closer to the performance date, we started watching full run-throughs so we could see the pieces of the show come together. After watching me do a scene with another actor, Claire approached me and took hold of my arm.

"That was really lovely work today, Anna," she said. Her eyes were sparkling. "No, I mean really wonderful."

I was thrilled, but something about the surprise in her voice made me feel like a monkey who had composed a sonata. Still, it was enough to make me reframe her in my mind as a strict but fair mentor of sorts.

We became almost friendly. We once walked to a Starbucks near Lincoln Center in the drizzling rain and didn't talk about work at all. I told her about my friends, who were all still in high school back home, and how I missed them but never knew what to say when we talked. She talked a little bit about her ex-husband (who was Philip fucking Roth, by the way) and her daughter, and like a typical seventeen-year-old I retained none of it. We were getting along well in spite of my fear and she seemed to have a growing respect for my *slightly* superior musicianship. I could read music and follow the time signature changes, which was especially important now that we were expected to listen for our cues instead of watching the conductor. The irony was that we were in the company of five full-time members of the New York City Opera, but their skill level so exceeded ours that we could almost no longer understand it to be impressive. It was like being the smartest janitor at NASA.

Claire had a rich voice and she acted the hell out of her songs, but she wasn't a confident musician—and not for nothing, Sondheim music is a damn battlefield. Our version of the show began with the curtain rising on a frozen tableau of the full cast. Claire's character sat before a wooden tray that was covered in playing cards and a brass handbell. I was seated on the floor by her feet, looking up at her. During the overture, Claire was meant to ring her bell to set all the characters in motion and begin the show. The cue had been a crapshoot during rehearsals, but in our final preview performance she missed it by enough that our conductor stopped the music entirely and went back to the start.

At the note session before opening night, our choreographer tentatively inquired if I could reach Claire's bell from where I was sitting in the opening tableau. I even more tentatively said yes. That settled that. We left the note session feeling a little awkward but relieved. I went up to the dressing room I shared with one of the NYCO members and started to get ready. Over the loudspeaker I heard the announcement, "Anna Kendrick to Claire Bloom's dressing room, Anna Kendrick to Claire Bloom's dressing room." That phrase still haunts my dreams.

I went down the four flights of stairs to her dressing room. She was set up in a solo room just off the stage and I inched to her door. She had her back turned when I slithered in, but she looked up and saw me in her mirror. She did not turn around.

"I told them I'm ringing the bell. I'm ringing the bell or I'm leaving the show."

If I hadn't been terrified, I would have found this kind of fabulous.

"When it's time, you are going to cue me. Just give me a nod, and then I will ring the bell."

"Okay," I squeaked.

I don't remember how I extricated myself or if she had me stay awhile and practice cueing her. But the image of her in that dressing-room mirror and her mannered phrasing are permanently burned into my brain. When I told my parents the story, my dad was shocked. "They just sent you to her dressing room? You're a *minor*; why the hell would they have you settle a dispute with an adult actress on your own?" It was a fair point, in retrospect.

I was happy to take all the criticism for even an ounce of praise, and if she ever reads this I hope my reverence for her is clear. But just in case it's not: Claire, I worship you. If I saw you tomorrow and you hit me in the face, it would be the highlight of my year.

She was the greatest living Shakespearean actress and I was a seventeen-year-old in a bad wig. I'm not just mitigating this because she happens to still scare the crap out of me, but because people being tough with you doesn't mean they're villains. Paul Gemignani kicked my ass on *High Society*, *A Little Night Music*, and *Into the Woods*, and that dude *loves* me. Right, Paul?

Does this wig make me look out of my depth?
Or is that just my face?

moving to la

I was told as a child that if I wanted to be in entertainment, I shouldn't have a backup plan. That is terrible advice. If things hadn't worked out for me, I'd be an Uber driver or the world's most prudish porn star. (Which doesn't mean I would be an *unsuccessful* porn star; there's a fetish for everything, ladies!) However, I'm glad I followed that terrible advice.

Don't get me wrong, I wish I had more skills, but if I'd had a safety net, I would have used it. Sometimes the terror was so overwhelming that if I'd been offered an apprenticeship scrubbing the floor of a button factory (what do normal jobs look like?), I would have thought, *Fine, I can't take this anymore—sign me up, give me the health benefits, give me a time card and a mean boss and some goddamn security.* I needed the fear. I needed to be forced to rely on myself, and the dream, and sometimes unemployment checks. (Thank you, US government! Please don't repossess my house when I go all *Grey Gardens*!)

It's obviously very lucky for me that, at the moment, acting is working out. This was not always the case. For a while there, if a casting director looked up from her clipboard, it was a good day. There are buildings in Los Angeles that still make me shudder when I drive past, the aura of rejection radiating off of them like a landfill on a hot day. I sometimes think that I should have a sense of pride knowing that I've achieved more than my sixteen-year-old brain would have ever let me imagine, but mostly it's just the opposite.

I think self-doubt is healthy. And having to fight for the thing you want doesn't mean you deserve it any less. Maybe I'm not supposed to mention that it was a fight, but I find that to be such an old-money attitude. I think I'm supposed to act as though I always knew I'd find success (not out loud, obviously—just using some heavy-handed subtext), but moving to Los Angeles felt like that dream where you're naked in a grocery store, hoping that no one will notice. I figured I'd be discovered and thrown out at some point. I'm still waiting.

I came to LA without a car. I was unprepared for the move in a lot of ways, and thinking I could walk to a grocery store and back before a carton of milk spoiled was a pretty glaring one. Why didn't anyone tell me you needed a car in LA? Because I didn't know a soul who lived there. That was a much greater problem, of course, but one thing at a time!

Craigslist apparently existed back then, but no one I knew had heard of it, so I found an apartment the old-fashioned way—getting an email, six people removed, about a woman looking for a roommate. I crafted a few paragraphs about what a responsible, tidy, and courteous person I was and sent it to the woman in question. Gwendolyn was in her mid-twenties, and although she was nervous about me being from out of town—she didn't want to babysit me—I assured her that I was very independent and I wouldn't rely on her while I got settled. After a couple weeks of correspondence, once all the details had been worked out, I mentioned that I was seventeen— SEEYOUINAFEWDAYSCAN'TWAIT!

The day I arrived Gwendolyn was cautious but welcoming, and I made sure to do my very best impression of a capable human as proof that I wouldn't be a burden. That day, I bought the cheapest desk and twin bed that Ikea made. For good measure, I got a couple of those ninety-nine-cent tea-light holders. I was taking Hollywood by storm and doing it in style.

I'd only ever seen two neighborhoods in Los Angeles, so I didn't know what a sketchy area I was living in. I ignored the fact that the corner store had bars on the windows and that there were prostitutes outside at all hours. My gruff, disabled neighbor was clearly renting out the abandoned car in the garage to a homeless man, and the woman below me had night terrors, but I had candle holders and I was going to be a goddamn actress.

I'd been paid a decent amount for a failed TV pilot before I officially moved to LA, but when every cent you make has to last until your hypothetical next job, you don't get comfortable. I had to stretch that paycheck indefinitely, but alas, I needed a car. I bought a used Toyota and named him Charlie, after Charlie Brown, because he broke down all the time.

The next pilot season was starting up, which meant I was usually sent on one to four auditions a day. I discovered Map-Quest and wrote down directions by hand since I didn't have a printer. Between that and my growing knowledge of the city, I was only getting lost, like, six times a day. Pilot season is grim because you're sent in for everything, no matter how wrong you are for it. I kept a mountain of clothes and accessories in my trunk so I could go from the fourteen-year-old goth daughter on a TNT drama to the spoiled twenty-two-year-old receptionist on a workplace comedy. It's obvious now that splitting my focus made it impossible for me to do well on any of them, but I was in no position to turn down auditions.

How do I describe my personal life during this time? I met funny, interesting people, I went to art galleries downtown, I performed a one-woman show for free on the street corner. Except none of that's true. I was alone and freaked out and I stayed in my room a lot. I spent most of my time trying to find ways to occupy myself without spending money or ingesting calories.

I didn't have any friends. Well, I didn't know anyone. Which is the less depressing way to say I didn't have any friends. I didn't know how to *make* friends in LA. Usually when people move to a new city, it's for school or for work. Unlike my friends who were entering college, I was not surrounded by packs of like-minded young people all equally eager to start new friendships. Unemployment and my lack of a fake ID were conspiring to turn me into a world-class recluse.

I managed to strike up a conversation with a girl in an audition waiting room once. She mentioned that she didn't have a ride home. Frankly, she seemed a little annoying, but I was desperate for human company, so I offered to drive her. (Fingers crossed that she's not crazy!) I immediately imagined telling people how my best friend and I might never have met if her car hadn't broken down that morning. (Eesh. Fingers crossed that

I'm not crazy.) In my car, I tried to play it cool. We made small talk; she said she'd grown up in LA, which made me doubly nervous. Then she rolled down the window, stuck her feet out, lit a cigarette, and changed the radio station. My new best friend was a real entitled bitch. I gave her my number when I dropped her off. She didn't offer hers in return.

Some young neighbors invited me to a party they were having. When they collected five dollars from everyone for pizza I nervously told them I didn't have any cash, but I would pay them back the next day. In the morning, I knocked on their door with my five dollars and they told me that someone had stolen the money. I assumed they suspected me. I'd been the only new person there. Did making a point to give my five dollars make me look more or less guilty? They assured me they didn't think I'd done it. I never spoke to them again. Does including this story in my book make me look more or less guilty?

When I was nominated for an Independent Spirit Award for *Camp*, I thought I might make friends with my fellow nominees. I also thought my parents would know what the Independent Spirit Awards were, but they've never been good at faking enthusiasm, so that phone call was disappointing. Whatever, this was going to be great! I didn't know how publicists or stylists worked, but I figured if you walked into a store at the Beverly Center mall and talked loudly about how you needed an outfit for a fancy award show, they'd offer you something eventually. That did not happen, but no worries, Anna, you're substance, not style; just focus on the art. I watched all the films from my category, some of which were not easy to track down. I thought this would facilitate conversation, but it ended up making me look like a superfan. I assumed my fellow emerging artists would have done their research as well. I guess they were busy effortlessly fitting in.

I tried to keep in touch with my friends from home. People I'd known since childhood were scattered at colleges around the country, but they all seemed to be having the same euphoric experience. I would call them and feel destroyed by loneliness. It was almost comical. Me sitting on my bed (trying not to disturb my adult roommate) as someone told me how amazing everything was and their new friends called out for them in the background. They had the next four years of their lives mapped out for them, and I was pretending I didn't see a homeless man asleep in the car next to mine.

I remember hearing somewhere that most people misremember their adolescence as entirely wonderful or (more often) entirely awful, when it was probably some combination of the two. My memory of my early time in LA suffers from this syndrome.

The first year *was* tough. I was lonely. I was broke. But things went from soul-crushing to tolerable in one evening. A friend of mine who was passing through LA took pity on me. He invited me to an *American Idol* viewing party with some of his friends. Most of the people there didn't know each other, and I bonded with two dudes named Peter and Alex over our shared outrage when Jennifer Hudson was kicked off. We started hanging out almost nonstop. After a few weeks, Peter and Alex mentioned that they both happened to be apartment hunting. I awkwardly said, "Can I come, too?" I think they were more than happy to have a girl around to make it clear that they were not dating.

(They *were* gay—in case the indignation over J. Hud's dismissal from *Idol* didn't tip you off—they just weren't dating each other.)

I told Gwendolyn via email and with minimal notice that I would be moving out. You know, like a coward! ☺ At that point I'd already been unmasked as a nonresponsible, nontidy, non-courteous person, so what did I have to lose? I disassembled my desk and bed and reassembled them in a three-bedroom apart-ment in West Hollywood. That moving day was glorious. I was eighteen and living with two dudes in an apartment with new carpet. I took the smallest bedroom, so I could pay fifty dollars less a month. The fact that it had only one, very small window gave the room a minimum-security-prison vibe, but we made a group trip to Ikea and this time I bought the *second*-cheapest dresser they made to class the place up.

The first week we lived there, Alex and I woke up to find tar tracked across the living room carpet. Peter had drunkenly stepped through a construction site, and wouldn't you know it—tar does not come out of carpet. Ever. I was pissed at Peter, but he was so lovable he got away with everything. It made the whole place look dingy and I had to nervously explain it away when I had anyone over. But we decided we'd rather lose the security deposit than pay to recarpet, so I attempted to hide the stain with an area rug. That decision essentially doomed the apartment to remain in its squalid state. But we figured we'd probably move in a year or so.

Alex and I were both under twenty-one, but Peter was of age and graciously bought alcohol for us. To save money on décor we exclusively drank Skyy vodka and artfully arranged the empty blue bottles in our living room. I hate day drinking now, possibly because it reminds me of this period. I think we drank just to feel like we were doing something.

For the most part, we had fun. We went to drag night at Micky's and someone dressed as my character from *Camp*, which made me feel more like a superstar than I ever have since. We got stoned and watched scary movies. I smoked too much the night we watched *The Amityville Horror* and climbed up the back of the couch begging the boys to stop reading my thoughts. It wasn't a great look, but this was the stuff that distracted me from the overwhelming uncertainty of my professional life.

A friend who worked at a catering company would occasionally need a temp last minute, pay me cash under the table, and let me have all the tuna Niçoise I could eat. But most of the time I was praying that *Law & Order* would need a mousy little teen killer so I could keep paying my car insurance.

Because Peter had lived in LA the longest and was old enough to go out at night, Alex and I became close, at first out of convenience and then out of genuine shared love of making fun of everything and everyone, most of all each other. We watched pop concerts on DVD. We tried to take edgy photographs of each other on my three-megapixel camera. We discovered the "casual encounters" section of Craigslist and, naturally, posted an erotic plea to meet up in the bushes at the end of our street. We waited outside until two guys showed up and walked off together. We were like the creepy cupids of anonymous sex.

Brazen little beasts that we were, Alex and I were not satisfied with just drinking in our apartment. We wanted to drink with the rest of the world! At that time, clubs were the pinnacle of Los Angeles nightlife. Maybe they still are and I'm just out of touch. Unlike bars, these clubs were large and open and played their music at horrifying volumes. I didn't know what went on in them, but I wanted to find out.

Alex knew a mysterious figure named Carlos who seemed to treat "going out" with the same urgency and focus as a mission from Homeland Security. The more I learned about LA nightlife, the more it seemed like a full-time job. Any decent subculture can sell you the promise that reaching the top of its hierarchy means you've accomplished something. Clubbing was no different. You went to the right club on the right night, which is to say you only went to the hardest clubs to get into, on the very hardest nights to get in. You spent all day primping and pregaming and all evening enjoying the fruits of your labor.

One night, Carlos asked us to meet him at Element, a name that inspired some reverence from Alex and, consequently, from me. We had to get in. We nervously explained to Carlos that while Alex had a fake ID, I did not. Carlos wasn't worried. He told us to come anyway. I assumed he was going to sneak us through some back exit, but when we arrived he walked straight toward the bouncer. Barely breaking his stride, Carlos said, "She's Ashley's best friend," and kept walking, dragging us behind him.

"Who's Ashley?" I asked.

"Ashley Olsen. I told the owner she was coming by tonight. She's not."

I was not twenty-one and neither was Ashley Olsen, yet her name had gotten a stranger through the door of a nightclub without question. The mention of fame in any form, even underage fame, cloaked me from suspicion. Personally, I was thrilled to hear the promise of her attendance was a ruse—I imagine if Miss Olsen had arrived I would have been thrown at her feet like the peasant I am and dragged out of the club.

The inside looked like a minimalist parody of itself. It was just a dark, empty space with black boxes laid out in different formations, serving as tables or chairs. The music was blaring.

"Why isn't anyone dancing?" I shouted.

If this had been the TV version of my life, a character would have explained that you don't dance, you just stand around looking cool. Unfortunately, people don't explain things like that in real life—they want you to shut up and blend in until you figure it out. Luckily for Carlos, the music was SO loud that he could reasonably pretend he hadn't understood me and trot away toward someone more interesting. Alex and I were left standing by ourselves. He seemed to immediately understand that we'd stumbled into some inner circle and playing along was the name of the game. I continued shouting.

"I don't get it; there's all this space, the music is too loud to have a conversation, but we're not supposed to dance? Are you just supposed to stand around looking at each other?" Alex was trying to telepathically communicate, *Yes, asshole, you are. Okay?*

I kept going. "Do they have to keep the music this loud because no one in Los Angeles has anything to say to each other?" I thought constantly making fun of LA made me look smart.

Alex ignored me and eventually I got the message that if I was so annoyed by the situation, I was free to leave. Sadly, the truth was that I was equally under the spell of the nightlife mythos. It didn't matter if you weren't having fun; you pretended that you were and bragged about it later. I wanted to do the bragging bit, so I shut my mouth and stayed.

For a while Alex and I engaged with the nightclub culture as frequently as we could. My interest in getting into these clubs didn't last long. (It would vanish completely after my twenty-first birthday because, like guys who play hard to get, or Tickle Me Elmo, or your first period, sometimes you only want a thing until you have it.) But at nineteen I did spend a short and regrettable period in a classic trap: trying to fit into something I hated, just to prove to myself that I could.

Once I realized (to my great relief) that Hollywood Party Girl was something I was not destined to be, I found increasingly joyous ways to spend my time.

Instead of privately obsessing over them, I forced Peter to help me rehearse audition scenes. The terrible roles were far more fun (and more frequent) than the good ones. The horror scenes were especially good fodder, and we'd end up screaming bloody murder and chasing each other around the apartment. It's weird that I never got those roles.

When some of my California-native friends heard I'd never been to Disneyland, they insisted on taking me that very moment, even though it was pissing rain. We ran around the park soaking wet but almost completely alone. I started teaching myself to bake, I went to an unreasonable number of costume parties—why

did my friends throw so many costume parties? I rediscovered my favorite things—long walks and great movies—and eventually the darkness and power that I'd projected onto the city started to dissipate. I hadn't booked a job or improved my financial situation, but I was going to be okay. Then a funny thing happened.

I started getting calls from the same friends from my hometown, the ones who'd been adapting so well to college, now in the first months of their sophomore year. Back at school again, they were no longer overwhelmed by newness or possibility. They had gone back to the same place, and the same friends—some of whom they had made hastily—and now they were lost. It was fine to be a freshman who hadn't declared a major, but now they had no idea what they wanted to do with their lives or what kind of person they wanted to be, and they were feeling the pressure to decide fast.

The role reversal was uncanny. I hadn't even booked a job yet, but somehow we'd switched places. I was convinced that I was on the right path, and they were riddled with uncertainty. I'd only been looking at the drawbacks of my situation; my single-mindedness meant that I had no backup plan, and I worried that if I failed, I'd be unhappy doing anything else. But now I saw this as a blessing. I knew what I wanted. I'd never considered how scared I would be if I didn't.

That year Felicity Huffman won an award for her work in *Transamerica* and said something in her acceptance speech that I held on to for years. "The second time I didn't work for a year, I gave up any dream that looked like this." It knocked me sideways. This undeniably talented woman went years without getting a job, not because she wasn't good, but because sometimes you just have to pass an endurance test. I worried that luck and timing and opportunity (and my little frame and goofy face) might never align at the right moments, but for all the inexorable insecurities that live inside my head, I knew what I was capable of. I just had to be patient.

I did get work, eventually. I acted in a few independent films that made me happier than I thought humanly possible, but they didn't change my financial situation or keep me all that busy. So I had to develop some hobbies.

My biggest time waster (and unrepentant money suck) was baking. Baking provided something I didn't know I needed: the ability to make something tangible. Actors don't *make* anything. You work all day but there's nothing physical to show for it. It's an oversimplification, sure, but it felt so rewarding to put a little effort into something and have three-dimensional evidence I could hold in my hands. It also provided more of a thing I've always liked: validation!

Baking is a really fun way to get people to like you. Being a good listener, a lively conversationalist, a loyal friend—it takes so much energy. Spend a couple hours alone in your kitchen and get the same effect? Sign me up! Sadly, I have less time for it now, but for a couple years, it was my whole identity.

When I was in the throes of my baking phase, my oven broke, and, luckily, different friends were happy to host me for a few hours and let me fill their apartments with the smell of cinnamon while I refused to let them help, because YOU DON'T KNOW THE SYSTEM. I saw baking as a risk-free way to try things that I knew were beyond my skill level. I was never the girl to strap on a snowboard and head straight for a black diamond, but if I saw "advanced" in the corner of a *Martha Stewart Living* recipe, I'd think, *Bring it on, you crazy bitch.*

This meant that I would sometimes spend hours in someone else's home, experimenting and cursing and emerging from the kitchen looking like I'd fought off a rabid cat. But my hazelnut torte would be shining and beautiful, and I'd go pawn it off on someone who hadn't seen behind the curtain and would praise me as a culinary genius.

One friend in particular liked having me come by. Scott wrote music during the day but didn't like being alone. He wanted someone around to chat with for a few minutes every hour or so but then needed to sit in front of his computer with headphones on to get work done. It became a semiregular arrangement. After about a year of this, he told me he'd gotten off meth. A month before.

What? What was he talking about? Meth addicts were gaunt and toothless; their hair was stringy and their nails were dirty and they certainly didn't burn me indie rock CDs. How could a friend of mine have been in this kind of trouble without me noticing? I felt foolish and so, so guilty. He was out of the woods (and sober ever since, thank god) but really, what kind of friend was I?

"So, you would just do it as soon as I left your apartment? I mean, were you ever like, *She needs to get out of here because I need to . . . do meth?*"

"No." He looked a little embarrassed, maybe more for me than himself. "I would do it before you got here."

"I've seen you on meth?!"

"I would say, for the last year, you've only seen me on meth."

I'm the biggest idiot on the planet.

"Yeah, I didn't like being alone, but then I just wanted to sit on my own and work once you got there. You really never noticed?"

"I thought that was just your personality!" I was reeling.

"Why do you think I never wanted to eat the food you were making?"

"You said you didn't have a sweet tooth! I believed you! Because, you know, I believe people when they say things!"

He was laughing now. I'd gotten shrill and frazzled. I was laughing with my friend about how he was hiding a meth problem from me. This is when I learned that I cannot tell when people are on drugs. At all.

After a while I met some fellow aspiring actors, which was nice because they were the only people in LA who didn't crack the old "So you mean you're a waiter" joke when the "What do you do?"

question came up. Every now and then we'd get stoned and talk about our silliest, most specific goals.

"I want the 'and' credit," someone would start. "You know, at the end of a bunch of credits sometimes there'll be a 'with' or an 'and.' Obviously I want to be a lead and get first billing or whatever, but someday I want to be the 'and' guy."

"Oh," I said, "I want the 'is a revelation.' Like in the *Brokeback Mountain* trailer when they show Michelle Williams and the voiceover guy reads a review like 'Williams is a revelation.' I want to be a revelation."

"That's a good one. Maybe I want that. No! I want the secret post-credits cameo!"

Most of my friends were not actors. A surprising percentage were just my neighbors. I became close with a group of stunning girls who lived in a duplex down the street. Paige was a model, Amy was an exotic dancer, and Valerie was a former exotic dancer whose wealthy boyfriend paid her bills and rent. They'd met during a lap dance. It was a true LA love story.

The girls were beautiful, hilarious, and tough as steel. On the night we met, Valerie, through her thick Queens accent, said, "You're smart, right? You know how I know you're smart? 'Cause I woulda copied offa you in high school."

I liked hanging out with them. These ladies could PARTY, and being with a group of girls that bombastic made me "the quiet one." I was their mousy, serious friend, and I happily leaned into the role. Surrounding myself with people who were so much more attractive than me meant I could feel like the substantial one. I wouldn't call it healthy, but I did it anyway.

They also had a talent for getting into and out of trouble. The cops showed up at their house once because of a noise complaint, and I swear on my life, they turned up the music, ran into the street, got on the cop car, and danced with the officers until they went away. In the rain.

We went to Vegas and Palm Springs. We went to the Spearmint Rhino in downtown LA after eating some especially potent pot brownies and watched Amy do what can only be described as an erotic Cirque du Soleil routine. When Valerie's boyfriend came into town, he'd rent out a suite at the Chateau Marmont and we'd all get drunk and choreograph fake music videos to every song on my iPod.

They got me out of the house, which was no easy feat. And no matter how hard I struggled, they forced me to occasionally have fun.

I still hadn't yet had a "boyfriend," though, and I realized this was unacceptably weird. Nineteen-year-olds had boyfriends, dammit. They had boyfriends, they had ex-boyfriends, most of them had multiple ex-boyfriends. I bought a book called *Guide to Getting It On!* and prepared to get it over with.

Outside of romance, my "real life" was coming together, slowly but surely. It didn't look like how I'd once thought it should. I couldn't afford Crate and Barrel plates (my ultimate idea of status. Related: Did you know that there are fancier places than Crate and Barrel to get plates??). The jobs I was getting were low-budget and almost willfully not mainstream. My friends weren't polished, but neither was I. It was so much better.

BOYS

boys and the terror of being near them

I read somewhere that the reason adolescent girls are attracted to androgynous young men is that they seem less threatening. Since their sexuality is not fully realized yet, they feel safer placing attraction on boys with thin frames and delicate features, because it subconsciously reminds them of another girl. They don't have to confront the implications of being attracted to someone masculine and virile enough to, you know, "do it." (Okay, I don't remember *exactly* what the thing said; I'm just trying to sound smart before I talk about "special feelings.")

The piece stuck with me, whether it had any merit or not, because I was totally one of those girls. I loved the baby-faced New Kids on the Block but felt wholly creeped out when they changed their name to NKOTB and started growing facial hair. When Jonathan Taylor Thomas cut his hair short enough that it no longer fell in his eyes, it was a betrayal. Zack Morris was far preferable to A. C. Slater. Slater was the one with the rippling muscles, but outside of lifting heavy furniture, what on earth did that have to do with anything?

The thing the article got wrong in my opinion was that I didn't feel threatened or intimidated by masculine guys; I felt nothing. They didn't stir something in me that I wasn't ready to deal with; they didn't stir anything at all. They seemed as attractive as the side of a building. Not that I knew exactly what I wanted to do with, say, Devon Sawa in *Casper*, either. Even my tender-faced teen crushes inspired pretty elementary goals. I knew I found them interesting, I knew I liked their faces, and I knew if we met (like if they maybe moved to Maine to escape the pressures of stardom) I'd want them to like me. Beyond that I wasn't sure what was supposed to happen. And once I found out, I was so nauseated that my daydreams would only reach the point where I kissed the object of my affection (a.k.a. the middle brother from *3 Ninjas*) before the dream cut out like a busted VHS and started again from the beginning.

I went through two phases of trying to win the affection of boys. While we were still young enough that sexual contact was off the table, I waged a full-out assault on the seemingly impenetrable interests of the male. I was short, I was loud, I wore the same thing to school for days at a time—where was I going wrong?

During that blissful period before I had to think about sex, I liked to present myself as "boy crazy." I did like boys, both boys that I knew and the appropriately feminine boys in *Teen Beat*, but I played up being "boy crazy" because it seemed like the trait of a pretty, popular girl. In third grade, I took a quiz in *Seventeen* magazine and brought it to school.

"I'm totally boy crazy according to this. It's so embarrassing. Look!"

I'd looked at the answer key prior to marking each question

but thought my classmates would be duly impressed. My teacher took a look at the magazine and cautioned me to curb this quality as I got older. *What is she talking about? The whole point of this is to seem like a cool, older girl!* It took me years to realize she was warning me not to become a slut.

For as much as I thought about boys, which wasn't as much as I pretended but was still a lot, they did not seem interested in holding up their end of the bargain. They were supposed to stride up to me in the cafeteria, push Libby Perrino and her shiny black hair to the side, and ask me to the school dance. But we didn't have dances in elementary school, and none of the boys I knew wanted to talk to me anyway.

Wait, that's it! By fifth grade, I cracked a major development in strategy. I needed to get boys to *talk* to me. I wasn't pretty, but I could make them like me through the magic of conversation, or at least trick them into revealing some actionable knowledge and go from there. My current crush was Matty Boothe. He had dirty-blond hair and seemed dangerous in that way that only a fifth-grade boy from Maine can. The only thing I knew about him was that he liked gory movies, so I spent a few weeks letting my older brother pick the movie rentals for a change. We'd tell our parents we got *FernGully* again and wait until they went to bed to sneak downstairs and watch his selection. I forced myself to sit through horror films and action films and *Pulp Fiction*. I knew I was unprepared to see some of them (*Pulp* fucking *Fiction*!) but I was going to turn myself into Matty Boothe's dream girl, dammit.

One day he stayed after class because he hadn't done his

homework (mah boy was such a rebel!), and I lingered and pretended to clean up my desk. I ever so casually struck up a conversation.

"Oh, Matty, you know the other day"—three weeks ago—"when you were talking about the grossest movies you'd ever seen?"

Cue Matty looking up at me, cautiously intrigued.

"Well, I've got a really gross one for you. Have you ever seen *Outbreak*?"

"*Outbreak* isn't gross. It's not even scary."

"Yeah, totally."

Okay, so talking to boys had not been a success. But I didn't blame myself for not watching movies that were gross enough or scary enough for this boy's taste. If anything, I walked away thinking, *Wow, talking to boys is not that fun. Or at least, talking to a boy with whom I have nothing in common, and who has no interest in me, is not that fun. New development! I just won't bother with boys who don't like me or any of the things that I like! I've learned my lesson and I'll definitely never make the same mistake again!*

In middle school, I discovered that liking boys who didn't like me back was all I'd be emotionally capable of for a very long time. Middle school was also when I went through a phase of liking exclusively non-Caucasian boys. They didn't like me back, either. Any boy of any ethnicity other than my own was automatically the object of my love. In case you forgot, we are in Maine at this point, and the handful of racially diverse young men I met in middle school immediately struck me as exceptional. I barely knew any of them; I was just attracted to them from afar. Looking back, it's pretty plain that what I liked was how different they seemed. I was desperate to be around anything and anyone outside of what I'd experienced in my life so far. One could even argue that I wasn't attracted to the *person* but was actually fetishizing their race (but definitely don't listen to that because it's dangerously close to an intellectually sound argument where I come off sort of racist). All I knew was that in sixth grade Shahin was beautiful and Iranian and so much cooler than me.

Seventh grade was interrupted when I moved to Yonkers with my dad for the duration of *High Society*, so I never developed a crush on anyone at school. In New York, I did have a crush on the boy who played Young Simba in *The Lion King*, but since I was only in a room with him one time and our parents were there, our love did not blossom.

My friend Nora from *The Sound of Music* and I often discussed that great mystery that looms before all adolescent girls: sex. We talked about sex A LOT. Not boys (I apologize if this freaks out any parents)—we did not talk about <3boys<3 and how cute Ryan's new haircut was, or how dreamy the boys in 98° were—we talked about sex. What we'd heard about it, what it would be like, how you were supposed to do it. We were on a mission to compile everything we'd ever heard about all things sex-related. Condoms, porn, hookers, first base, second base, third base, and by the way, when the hell were we gonna get boobs?

If any parents are still with me, the good news is that we were way more interested in figuring it out than actually doing it. We were like theoretical sex engineers. Oh! *Theoretical Sex Engineer*! Title of my next book!

The other good news is that we were pathetic. We were the blind leading the blind. She told me about a pornographic comic book she'd seen and the offensive joke it contained about Hispanic women's pubic hair. I told her that a girl from my church had seen Stephen King's *Thinner*, and in one scene, the wife leaned in to her husband's lap and moved her head up and down. . . . So blow jobs involved . . . moving, I guess?

It's adorable in a super-uncomfortable way, right?

I'm grateful that we were wondering the same things and that we were both hungry to put a name to our feelings and to have someone reflect them back. I didn't know how lucky I was until I went home and received many blank stares from friends who were not interested in or prepared for talking about sex out loud.

That was the last time I would ever be ahead of the curve sexually. In fact I pretty much plateaued there for the next six years. This was only a noticeable problem once I got to high school and phrases like "fooling around" and "hooking up" were no longer empty braggadocio.

When kids I knew started to go past first base, I felt nervous and excited. It was like waiting in line for a roller coaster, if you'd seen a sex-ed video about how the roller coaster was probably going to ruin your life. For me, the nervousness usually outweighed the excitement. Now that potentially seeing each other naked was part of the package, I would still try to court the male, and then RUN FOR MY LIFE at the smallest sign of interest. I was the romantic equivalent of the annoying friend who goes to the haunted house but chickens out and eats candy apples outside until it's over (also me).

I don't know if my aversion came from the suspicion that I'd make a fool of myself, insecurity about my body, or just the fear that it would hurt. I could sense I wasn't anatomically ready when most girls were; maybe the emotional part was waiting for the physical part to catch up? It certainly wasn't that I didn't have The Feelings. But I was dealing with those on my own.

I was conflicted, to say the least, and it didn't help that I'd found a pamphlet under a seat in the auditorium that proclaimed, "No one likes a tease," but I still sought to ensnare a boy. Sure, the odds were against me, but there had to be at least one guy I could trick into settling for a girl who wore a training bra and was terrified of sex.

There was Andy, who had long eyelashes and was so cerebral and self-aware that even at fourteen I deemed him "pretentious." Intellectual insults were my high school version of pushing someone on the playground. If I thought he deserved the label, it clearly didn't bother me very much. I followed him around during his free period so often I almost failed the class I was *supposed* to be in during that time block. We flirted a lot and kissed a few times, and I was never sure if we didn't get together because he didn't want to, or because I would get that queasy "what if he wants to see me naked" feeling whenever he showed more than a passing interest.

I met Hunter at a rave that my brother snuck me into. He was slight and kind of gorgeous. He wore a bandanna with the

Puerto Rican flag, I suspect to compensate for his misleading white-kid name, and he told my friend Lindsey that I had a "nice ass." Who talked like that? Even putting that memory on paper gives me butterflies. I had never met anyone so forward. He asked for my number (what are we, in a movie?) and called a couple times but stopped after the third phone call when the awkward pauses led him to ask, "Am I bothering you?" *No, you're not bothering me! This is the most exciting thing that's happened to me ever!*

But I didn't say that. I was stuck in the limbo of wanting a fifth-grade relationship but not being able to admit it, even to myself. I mean, I wanted to do *something* before I graduated, but not everything. And the only thing worse than having sex or being a virgin loser forever would be having a mature conversation with a guy I liked about waiting until I was ready. The world would have ended.

Even though I remember high school as a never-ending barrage of rejection, I would feel dishonest if I didn't acknowledge that there were guys who liked me. Or at least one. Noah left a rose by my locker on Valentine's Day and had to trick me into walking past it, because my locker was on the third floor and I didn't use it. I panic-hugged him, said "No thank you," and walked away before I had to look at his face. He was remarkably cool about it and made sure things didn't get weird. We stayed close friends throughout high school, and when he asked me on a Friday, "You wouldn't want to go to prom on Saturday, would you?" I wrongly assumed the late ask and casual tone meant "as friends." I was grossed out and frankly kind of hurt when he drove me to a motel after the dance. I had to pull the old phone call to Mom where I loudly whine "Why not?" and say my mom's being a bitch and I have to go home. (An excellent tool for getting kids out of situations they don't want to be in. My mom always played along and I would recommend this trick to any parent.)

Some bitter boys reading this might accuse me of "friend-zoning," but I'd like to say that even if a girl has misinterpreted a situation that someone else thinks was obvious, she does not owe her male friends anything.*

Noah knew me well. He knew I was a virgin, in every possible sense, and that I didn't take it lightly. But the motel implied that he hoped we could fool around, even though we weren't dating. He was a nice boy who did something skeezy, and it sucked. We stayed in touch for a while after I moved to LA. In fact, he and a friend once stayed on my couch for a week and left a lovely thank-you note on the refrigerator the morning they left. I woke up and saw the note and felt guilty for being irritated by the end of the visit. Then my roommate stuck his head out of our bathroom. "There's an enormous shit sitting in the toilet." Maybe you're just destined to lose touch with some people.

---

* Needless to say, this applies to every arrangement of gender and orientation. I mention males pressuring females because that's been my only personal experience of it, but it turns out my personal journey isn't an infallible barometer of the entire human experience. Weird, right?

i guess we're doing this,
or how does this scene end?

I met Landon through the internet. Not ON the internet like some kind of freak. No, I met him the normal way: Heather (my hot blond friend) met Brent (Landon's hot blond friend) on Myspace and those two introduced us right around the time they were getting tired of having hot blond dry-humping sessions. Because hot blonds need break-up wingmen, I guess?

Landon was attractive and he knew *Anchorman* by heart, which at the time passed for really funny. He was kind of a jock, which made me want to turn my nose up at him—as I did with all jocks—so I could let the world know that not being with a handsome, athletic type was MY CHOICE. But he was persistent and a genuine romantic, and when I weighed my options logically it seemed silly not to date him. I wanted to escape the wasteland of being the nineteen-year-old loner and, to the naked eye, this guy was perfect. He was polite and punctual and my friends liked him a lot . . . and he was very handsome.

One day during our courtship, he dropped off a novelty trucker hat on my doorstep. I know we've all figured out that novelty trucker hats are hideous, but it was cool at the time.

Today, that would be like a guy giving you a spiked ear cuff, or a turtleneck crop top (or for future editions: a novelty trucker hat, because fashion is cyclical). It was sweet and original and I could resist no more. Let's be real: he had a pulse and he wanted to be my boyfriend.

On our first official date, he took me to a trendy restaurant. I rolled my eyes over how "LA" it all was. I'd never been somewhere so stylish, which should have made me nervous, but being openly disdainful of anything cool *is* in my comfort zone, so I still had a couple moves at my disposal. I really shine in a Taco Bell parking lot with a water bottle full of vodka, but I could work with this.

After dinner, we went back to my apartment and talked with my roommates for an appropriate length of time before retiring to my room and crawling into the luxury of my twin bed. We fooled around for a while, I employed a few suggestions from the early chapters of the *Guide to Getting It On!*, no one recoiled in horror at any point—a successful first-date-level encounter.

I got up to go to the bathroom, and when I came back, the first thing that went through my mind was *Why is he still here?* I was thrilled! I was proud of myself. I was still in control! Just because we'd hooked up didn't mean he had the upper hand. I was still powerful, and hard-hearted, and I could walk away from this whenever I felt like it.

The next morning, we drove to breakfast and I told him as much, just so he knew the score. "Okay, creepy," he said, and turned up the radio.

I assessed the situation. We'd had a nice dinner, some playful banter, and fooling around that was in no way objectionable. All right, world, let's do this, let's have me a damn boyfriend.

I looked at dating him as a kind of personal experiment. Something about him being a jock or liking nice restaurants or having the stench of family money despite his studio apartment made me feel like this would be a safe bet for me. In theory, I should have been intimidated. Instead, I felt superior. He'd also never met a girl as bossy as me, and knowing that emboldened me even more. *I am a boss bitch, and this dude is too basic to hurt me.* Neither of those slang terms were around yet, but that's the vibe I had.

I am a jerk for feeling superior to anyone ever, and that was equally true of Landon (despite being the kind of guy who saved up to buy the exact suit Ashton Kutcher wore on the cover of *GQ*). I made fun of him *a lot*—luckily that's the kind of thing that comes across as playful at nineteen—but Landon turned out to be fun, caring, and seriously right-brain smart.

After a satisfactory couple of months, I felt more committed to this "dating experiment" and started subconsciously, and sometimes consciously, making a bizarre coming-of-age checklist. (Had I learned nothing from my beads-and-lipstick pen pal episode?) It was mostly stuff I'd seen in movies, and I knew it was stupid, but every milestone gave me a sense that I was approaching normalcy. Nothing in my life was going especially well at that point, but if the guy I was seeing burned a CD for me (Check!) it felt like I was becoming a standard American adult.

He asked me to take a road trip to meet his parents.

"Okay. If I meet your parents, would that make us boyfriend and girlfriend?"

"I thought we already were boyfriend and girlfriend."

"No, we're not. But would you agree that me 'meeting your parents' would make us officially boyfriend and girlfriend?"

"Yeah, creepy, I guess it would."

"Okay, great. I'm looking forward to it."

The road trip hit a lot of items on my imaginary relationship checklist. We shared painful childhood memories during the long stretches of the drive—Check! We took pictures kissing in front of national landmarks—Check! He showed me his child-hood bedroom—Check! It was like a real relationship! All of it was genuinely meaningful to me, but the checklist was always there, giving me little bonus rushes of validation.

After I met his parents and we got back to LA, I addressed a big unchecked box. "Okay, we're boyfriend and girlfriend now. So we should have sex, right?"

Landon had had sex before and always assured me that he was fine with what we were doing. Gently, he said, "I'd love to, but only if you want to, and if you think you're ready." He put his hand on my arm.

"Blechhhh. Don't make this weird, let's just go have sex."

Sex was GREAT!! Why hadn't anyone told me?! I mean, it hurt. It actually hurt a lot, and not just for a "moment" the first time (I'm lookin' at you, "erotic novels"). But, okay, it was crazy! Sex wasn't like the other stuff at all!

Each time we'd finish (actually the first few times no one "fin-ished" per se, but, you know, we'd *stop*) I'd talk a mile a minute:

"God, I wish I could explain what it feels like, but I can't put it into words 'cause, like, a person is IN my body. You are IN my body. And I'd never really thought about it, but nothing's ever been IN my body before, you know? Like, I can't just open a hatch in my leg and put something in there, you know? What does it feel like to you?"

"It feels really good."

"Ugh, that's not what I mean. You are the worst. Tomorrow can we try a different position?!"

I felt alive. I didn't just feel different, I felt like I had super-powers. And I definitely felt like I was in the club. I saw a cool-looking girl in line at Starbucks and thought, *I'll bet that girl has sex. And I have sex, too. We get it. Like, I could go up to her and be like,* Oh, hey, do you have sex? *and she'd be like,* Yeah, *and I'd be like,* Yeah, me too. I totally know what it feels like.

The sex checklist was the most egregious of all. Most people I knew had been at it for years now, and I needed to catch up. I wanted to check off all the greatest hits. I barreled through every cliché, and it turned out a lot of it wasn't that sexy, but we both pretended that it was. We did the blindfold thing, we did the whipped-cream-and-chocolate-sauce thing, I bought a tacky red bustier for Valentine's Day and fuzzy green handcuffs for St. Patrick's. Oh, and the *Guide*! I put that baby into well-organized action. When Landon would question something, I'd pull out the *Guide* and point out that according to a book I bought in a West Hollywood thrift store called Out of the Closet, plenty of couples do it.

Shower sex—Check! Sex with ice—Check! Sex in the back of a parked car like teenagers in a movie about the 1950s—Check!

I wanted to ask if he was circumcised, because I couldn't tell, but my roommate Peter told me, "Dude, you can't ask him that. *Don't* ask that." I don't know why I wasn't allowed to ask, I guess because it would make me look stupid, or make him uncomfortable, but I didn't know how else I was supposed to find out. (After we broke up I didn't see another penis for a year and by that time I couldn't retroactively compare the two, so I still don't know.) Aside from that, I was in the trenches, having fun and learning a lot. Landon and I were both more interested in the other person's pleasure, not because we were selfless people, but because we got validation from it. It led to some energetic but fruitless evenings.

Anyway, the sex was a blast and the relationship was going great! Well, it was going okay. Well, it was tolerable. At the end of the day, we were just incompatible (which we wouldn't figure out for a few more months) and better off as friends (which we wouldn't figure out for a year after breaking up). But c'mon, we were living the dream: going on coffee runs in the morning, finding ways to kill time in the afternoon, and having sex before bed. Being normal!

About four months into dating, we were casually having the kind of philosophical conversation that no nineteen-year-olds should be allowed to have without supervision, and Landon said, "Well, sex before marriage is a sin."

At this point, in my opinion, religion played a convenient

role in Landon's life. The hypocrisy bothered me and I liked to debate him on it. This was so flagrant it was delicious.

"Excuse me? Then what the hell have we been doing?" Guys, I wasn't even that mad, it was just too silly for words.

"Well, no, I mean I *used* to believe sex before marriage was a sin. Now I think it's okay as long as the people are in love."

"I'm not in love with you. We've never said 'I love you.' Are you in love with me?" Admittedly, I wasn't exactly setting him up to say it, even if he had been.

"Um, okay, no, but we care about each other." I rolled my eyes. He was digging himself to China. Then he said, "And you always initiate it."

I stared at him.

"What does that mean? What is that? Some Adam and Eve temptation complex?" (A term I made up on the spot.) "Are you saying you want to be having less sex? Or just that when we have sex, it's my fault? Need I remind you that you'd slept with *seven* girls before we met?"

"I'm just saying that it's one thing if we can't help ourselves. You don't have to be so, like, ready and willing. I'm not saying we wouldn't be having sex at all, it's just you don't always have to initiate it."

"So, what, you'd prefer it if I had to be . . . *convinced*?"

He chose his words carefully. "Okay, it's just that the chase is kind of gone. It's kind of a turnoff."

Huh, I thought, *I wonder how much therapy I'll need to undo the damage from this moment.*

The origin of his logic had taken a turn, but I couldn't even be bothered to point it out. The behavior that I'd thought was adventurous, and awesome, and earning me girlfriend-of-the-damn-century points was making him lose interest in fucking me because I seemed too . . . available? Three months ago I was terrified of being outed as the virgin freak. Now I'd had sex with all of one person and somehow I was getting slut-shamed.

I'm not interested in pretending to be a reluctant participant because you think girls who like sex are a turnoff. If you think girls are supposed to object to sex until they find themselves incapable of resisting your magic penis, fuck you. (Unless this is a role-play fantasy between consenting adults, in which case I'll go to the Wizarding World of Harry Potter and grab some props right now.)

We fought for a while, he backtracked a lot, and we made up. I don't think he meant for it to make me feel the way that it did. Honestly the worst thing that happened was I wrote some truly appalling poetry about it.

No one was going to make me think women were supposed to hate sex. I knew I was right, which is a comfortable place for me, even when I'm really pissed off. But it rattled me. I found it troubling, because I wondered if other guys felt the same way.

We didn't last much longer. He drove to my apartment one afternoon—on a day that I had miraculously bothered to do my hair and makeup—and said he felt like it wasn't working anymore. At first, I thought I could just ignore that it was happening. I kept going about business in my room. "You're right, I need to make more of an effort. We should hang out with your friends more, I know that."

"No, I don't think that's it. I just think— Can you sit down?"

Okay. Crap. We're really doing this. And it sucks. But at least I look half cute.

Our relationship had started as an experiment in adulthood, but I was really invested now (Oh! Real emotional investment— Check!) and he was dumping me. Deep breaths. Obviously, a breakup wasn't on my checklist, but I wanted to make the best of a bad situation.

"So," I said, "what happens now?" He was giving me this horrible concerned face. The pity stung worse than the rejection. I wanted to punch him.

"Well, we can stay friends if you want. I know I'd like to. But I'll understand if you—"

"No, I mean what happens *right* now. Like, how do you finish a breakup? Like . . . how does this scene end?"

(Okay. A word here: I'm not some sociopath who can't tell the difference between real life and a movie. I was just using "scene" to differentiate the immediate situation from our hypothetical future dynamic. That said, my deliberately robotic demeanor probably confirmed that he was right to cut and run.)

He'd gotten the ball rolling; I wasn't planning to change his mind. I just needed to know how to wrap it up. Still, he was taken aback.

"Um . . . I don't know. Do you want me to stay for a while?"

"So we can make 'pity' faces at each other for half an hour? I'd rather you just leave." I was being vindictive, but give me a break, I was getting dumped.

"Okay . . ." He was doing a good job of looking appropriately bewildered by my callous response. *Whatever*, I reasoned, *I totally let that guy off the hook. Easiest breakup ever.*

I cried after he left. And it wasn't just something I needed to "get under my belt." It sucked. And my ego hurt. That night my roommates stayed home with me. We watched bad movies and ate cookie dough straight from the tube and talked about what a jerk my ex-boyfriend was—Check!

I went ahead and hated Landon passionately, but only because I thought it was another requirement of my relationship experiment. If you'd asked me about him while we were still dating, I doubt I would have said, "I can't get enough of him and I feel great about where our relationship is heading."

Half of my brain knew it was a blessing. The other half screamed, "How dare he dump me?!" That feeling only lasted about a week, and then I got comfortable knowing that I had an "ex-boyfriend." Talking about "my ex" was just another thing that normalized me, so I counted it as a win.

The lingering confusion about how liking sex with my boyfriend could be a turnoff messed with me for a little while, but no more so than the virgin/whore stuff that's everywhere in our culture. The hard part is that Landon is a good guy, and sometimes good people can still hurt each other.

I didn't have sex again for a year, but based on who I was hanging out with during that period of my life, I doubt I missed anything spectacular. Lesson for young men: if you want your eventual wife to be excited about sucking your dick for forty years, don't create a generation of women who think enthusiasm about sex is a bad thing.

I ran into Landon about a year after we broke up and immediately realized I didn't hate him at all, and we've been close friends since. His favorite thing to do is drag me to Starbucks even though he knows I don't drink coffee anymore. My favorite thing to do is whisper "He beats me" to the barista when Landon turns his back. He does not find it funny at all.

I went to his wedding last year. When his wife walked down the aisle he cried his ass off. It was beautiful. During the ceremony, the minister talked about having a healthy sexual relationship and how the marital bed was a place for love and honesty and respect, and I was glad that religion and intimacy were finding balance in Landon's life. Then Pastor "Marital Bed" McGee expounded on the subject for another seven minutes and made everyone tremendously uncomfortable.

I caught up with his parents and his bride. I took pictures of the newlyweds on my phone, as though they weren't going to have enough. I refused to dance.

I said my good-byes and walked through a gorgeous field toward my car. Everything seemed wonderfully strange. I'd just been to "my ex's" wedding, and I was content in the knowledge that he was so happy and found such a good fit.

(Check.)

he's just not that interesting

The summer I turned twenty-one I dated a musician named Connor. Well, I thought he was a musician and that we were dating. He thought he was a screenwriter who occasionally played music and that we were "hooking up and not labeling things because labels cause drama." He was twenty-eight and something of an introvert. I took this to mean that he was deep and artistic and probably judged me for talking as much as I do. Once we broke up I realized it just meant that he was kind of boring. And probably judged me for talking as much as I do.

This was my first lesson in He's Just Not That Into You. Sure, that episode of *Sex and the City* had aired and the book had been written, but guess what, TV writers can't learn your life lessons for you. I plowed ahead, actually having conversations with friends that sounded like this:

"Do you think I'm coming across overeager? Do I need to play it more cool with him?"

"Maybe? Why don't you just not call him for a while and wait for him to get in touch with you?"

"Well, if I didn't call him *at all* we'd never talk again."

(Oh. Sweet Anna.)

When we first started hooking up, I was twenty. He would play in clubs and bars at night, which meant that at first, it was simply unavoidable that he'd spend most of the night without me and invite me over once he got home. I reasoned that it wasn't a booty call if the law was keeping us apart. A fake ID was out of the question, since I looked like a guilty fifth grader on my best day. So at a certain point my only goal became to not get dumped before I turned twenty-one; *then* I'd be able to really get my hooks in. Oh god, it hurts to write.

Looking back, it's hard for me to understand what I was doing. Why on earth would I pursue someone who clearly had no interest in me? It's not like we had *fun* together; the man didn't *like* me so much as tolerate me. I suppose the easy answer is that I hadn't had a decent relationship yet, so I thought bagging a "cool" and attractive male was the whole objective. We would have made a terrible couple. But his indifference blinded me to all the red flags. He drove a BMW but slept on a futon. He watched the History Channel like it was a reliable source of information. Part of me knew I was only determined to bring him around because he was resisting me, but the idea of acknowledging the rejection hurt more than pretending it might be going somewhere.

I'd been so nervous when we met (and only got increasingly nervous as I tried to win his affection) that as a result, I have no idea what I was even like around him. If I could see tape of us interacting, I doubt I'd recognize myself. Who was I supposed to be making him fall in love with? My strategy was to just be agreeable. I had this fantasy of a braver, parallel-universe version of myself, but I was the most sterile, inoffensive version instead.

When he said things to me like "You use humor as a defense mechanism," I *should* have said, "Yeah, and you use pithy proclamations that let you maintain your sense of superiority as a fuckin' defense mechanism." Instead I clenched my teeth and made a plan to be more serious from then on.

We saw each other sporadically. Sometimes I'd send a breezy text, start a casual conversation, and spend the day staring at my phone until he got the hint and invited me over. Our group of mutual friends would get together a couple times a week and I'd invariably end up going home with him after those nights, so I did not miss one group hang-out that summer. At the time this group seemed impossibly cool to me as well. I'm sure their allure was wrapped up in my desire to stay connected to him. Also, I don't know if being motivated by amazing sex would have made my desperation more pathetic or less, but I cannot say that was part of it.

Nothing about the sex was bad, but after a month or two, I still hadn't, you know . . . arrived. (Mom, I'm sorry, but I told you not to read this chapter! If you're seeing this, it's your own fault!) Obviously, in my pitiful state, I wasn't disturbed by this orgasm drought for *myself*, but for HIM. I assumed that if I wasn't enjoying myself enough he'd end up feeling discouraged and less interested in doing it at all. If he was rocking my world, he'd want to do it more, right? For all I know, he wouldn't have noticed if I'd turned to stone mid-thrust, but I figured it couldn't hurt. So. No masturbation. Cut out all solo activity. I just won't climax for so long that eventually he'll have to make me.

Six weeks went by. SIX WEEKS. And I was getting *nothing* supplementally speaking. I was sticking to my guns. I was the master of my domain. Finally, I went to his apartment one night and I knew it was going to happen. I was on a hair trigger. (SIX WEEKS.) Oddly enough—or not odd at all since I hadn't come in six weeks—I got there during actual sex, which had never happened before. Now, creepy sex checklist aside, I was pretty damn inexperienced at this point, so this wasn't some huge accomplishment, it was more like a statistical inevitability. As we lay on his futon, I thought I'd tell him.

"So hey, first time I've had an orgasm during that whole situation." I raised my hand for a high five. "Up top!" He chuckled sardonically and shook his head.

"You know, you could say, like, 'Wow, I've never had an orgasm from doing that before, you're the first.' It should be a nice thing to hear."

Was this dude using his therapist voice to tell me how to better stroke his ego after sex? I should have said, "I haven't come in six weeks. A mammogram could have brought me to screaming orgasm, so you really shouldn't be smug." But instead I clenched my teeth and scolded myself for ruining this moment I'd worked so hard for.

As the weeks went on, I alternately gained and lost ground. He had some setbacks professionally and he opened up to me about some of his fears and insecurities. *This is awesome,* I thought gleefully as I held him.

A couple of weeks later he was still feeling down. I offered to come over early one morning and cook him breakfast. This was partially a gesture, something to make him feel cared for, and partially because he was so strapped for cash I knew he'd appreciate a free batch of groceries. He'd taught me how to make his favorite breakfast burrito and I went to the Gelson's Market by my apartment to pick up everything we needed. Normally, I walked to Gelson's every morning to buy a lone Power Bar. But today the checkout girl saw my basket: the tortillas, the eggs, the spices. She noted the change in my purchase and commented, "Trying something new?"

"Oh! Yeah . . ." I paused. "I'm making breakfast for my boyfriend." What was the harm in saying it, right? It felt like Connor and I were probably heading there anyway, and as far as she knew I was perfectly deserving of having the guy I'd been seeing for months accept the title of "boyfriend." Unlike, say, all my friends, this girl had no reason to believe I was kidding myself. She smiled back at me and nodded conspiratorially. *Yes,* I thought, *it is adorable. How quaint am I, clumsily attempting to cook breakfast for my boyfriend? Like something out of a movie, I'd burn the first batch, he'd laugh, and I'd smack his arm. Yes, Gelson's lady, that's exactly what's going on here.*

I made the breakfast and he was grateful, but it wasn't quite how I'd pictured it. We fooled around and he made another helpful suggestion for how my post–blow job behavior could be more affectionate or make him more comfortable or some shit. He had somewhere to be that afternoon, so we both headed out. I was in the car, waiting to make a left-hand turn, when my phone rang. It was him! He never called me first! Especially not so soon after saying good-bye. I snatched the phone out of the cup holder and answered. "Hi, stalker, just can't leave me alone, can you?" Nice one, Anna, perfect play.

"I was just behind you. You're doing my most hated thing. When people turn left onto Sweetzer but don't signal, so no one knows why you've stopped. I just had to go around you."

I thought he was calling to say thank you for breakfast, or tell me something funny he'd just seen that made him think of me, or maybe just to say that it was nice to see me and could we hang out again tonight. He was calling to critique my driving.

Why was I trying to spend more time with this person?! I didn't even enjoy his company! What is wrong with twenty-year-old girls?!

I debated even telling this part of the story because I hate admitting that I forgot to signal. But on the upside, it shows what a spineless doormat I was shaping up to be, so it stays!

When I finally turned twenty-one it didn't change our dynamic as much as I had hoped it would. He started showing interest in a new girl in the group named Erika, and I could feel him pulling away even more. The next time we had a vague talk about "what we were doing," he seemed to debate himself Sméagol/Gollum style in front of me. "Well, we get along . . . I mean, we don't ever fight . . . and I'm not saying that I want to be with anyone else right now . . . but I guess I don't want to miss out on any opportunities." I should have screamed, "I'M the opportunity, you asshat!" But I clenched my teeth and convinced myself once again that I didn't need a "label." Before I left, I at least managed to ask the question.

"Okay, so you don't want to be with someone else, but I have to ask. . . . Erika . . . is there anything there I should be worried about?"

He furrowed his eyebrows, more in comic surprise than anger.

"Erika the brunette? Barrett's friend? No, no, I'm not even attracted to that girl—I think that girl has a boyfriend." It was enough for me. I figured a guy who secretly liked a girl might protest that she had a boyfriend as a cover-up, but if he hoped they might get together at some point he wouldn't bother saying he wasn't attracted to her or call her "that girl." Twice.

(Yes, reader, I know you know where this is going. You are far better at everything than I am.)

A few weeks later he came over and broke up with me. I cried. So much. It was hideously embarrassing. What had happened to me? I had handled my first breakup like a champ. This guy so obviously wasn't into me, we weren't ever really together in the first place, and I was behaving like a messy trophy wife who'd just been told the prenup was ironclad.

He was very sensitive about it and put up with a lot of waterworks from a girl who'd claimed over and over she was fine with just "having fun." During the following days, the finality of being dumped started to feel like a relief. It could have gone on like that for god knows how long—being ignored, making myself available, swearing I was fine with how things were, too nervous to push for the "boyfriend" status. Or worse, I could have actually transitioned it into a real relationship—I've seen it happen. It looks miserable. I always want to scream at the guy, "You let her get her hooks in so far that you *married* her? Did you even notice it happening??" And I want to scream at the girl, "This is what you put in all that work for? A husband who's utterly disinterested in you and cheats constantly while you turn a blind eye??"

Almost immediately after we ended it, I could see that I was far angrier with myself than I was with Connor. On one hand, he must have seen I was more invested than he was, and arguably he should have let me down easy in the first few weeks of knowing me. On the other, I can't blame a guy for believing me (or more likely, pretending to believe me) when I insisted I was happy keeping things low-key and having casual sex.

I left town a few weeks later to film an independent movie in a tiny town in Indiana. After work one night, I logged into Myspace on the slow motel internet. I'd held out on cyberstalking for a while (two days) and rewarded myself by looking up Connor and everyone remotely connected to him.

In modern movies, the dumped girl finds out about the new girlfriend through a picture: the dude and his new girlfriend smiling on a hike or kissing at a party. I found out because Erika wrote a blog post about it. There, on Myspace, was a half-page post about the new man in her life. The most surreal part was that she'd incorporated lyrics from his songs throughout, like sappy, stilted Mad Libs. You wouldn't know those songs, so I won't try to re-create her post, but imagine if Paul McCartney had a new girlfriend and she wrote something like this online: *I knew that If I Fell it would be a Long and Winding Road, but Do You Want to Know a Secret? I need him Eight Days a Week, because All You Need Is Love.*

I thought my skull was going to cave in on itself.

Thank the lord that at this point in my life I'd implemented my "no matter how upset you are, sleep on it" policy regarding conflict. I drafted ten different emails to Connor. They ranged from furious, wounded, two-page diatribes to the classic single "Wow." It's a dangerous word to send an ex. Ostensibly restrained and dignified but in reality self-righteous and petulant. I slept on it and in the end sent nothing.

My poor coworkers in Indiana never heard the end of it. Despite my moaning, the cast and crew were really supportive. They didn't know the situation, they had no obligation to cheer me up, but on days I was mopey the director would say, "My landlord back in LA just called and told me there's a toothless prostitute named Erika—with a 'k'—hanging out behind the dumpster in our alley and she's offering hand jobs for a dollar, but no one's taking her up on it."

"You've never even seen a picture of her. I know you're trying to make me laugh, but she's actually really pretty."

"You're right. She's very pretty for a toothless prostitute who hangs out behind dumpsters and smells like a pile of dead rats. Oh yeah, he said she smells like a pile of dead rats."

It's amazing the way this over-the-top and uncalled-for meanness warmed my loathsome little heart. It's a strategy I've followed, perhaps at my peril, when my friends go through similar scenarios.

I know it's childish and lame, but it feels good, and you're allowed to be a miserable shit for a while after you get dumped. You know your ex and his new girlfriend aren't evil, but it's easier to feel like they are. Breakups can turn fully dimensional people into stubborn little vessels for your most stubborn little feelings. It takes a while for them to change back.

Very recently a strange thing happened. Someone who still knows Erika brought her up to me. I cringed: *that bitch.*

"You know she still thinks you're pissed at her." This gave me pause. She still thinks what? How does she even know me? I was twenty, I was a mousy girl she met one time. I assumed she hadn't even caught my name. I figured she didn't know I was a person. But I realized, *Oh my god, I'm not pissed at her. I'm SO not pissed at her. I literally have no feelings about her. In fact I don't think I'd recognize her if I fell over her!* Oh, hello, fully dimensional human, you're free to leave my brain now!

It was a real lesson in my endless capacity to hold a grudge. I do it so well, I don't even notice that it's happening. I walk around with these calcified resentments for years until someone points them out and I can go, "Good lord, is that still in here? Let's get rid of that. And throw out 'pretending that watching boys play video games is fun' while we're at it."

I had to take a moment to wonder who else fell into this category of default enemy. I went through a mental list of people who, in theory, I'd want to hit in the face with a meat tenderizer. My coworker from ten years ago who owes me like three grand? It was ten years ago! You were addicted to OxyContin! Go! Be free! My seventh-grade teacher, who told me that most child actors don't succeed as adult actors? You just wanted to scare me into having a backup plan! Farewell! Good luck! Tori from fourth grade, who accused me of writing mean stuff about all our friends on the playground wall? BURN IN HELL, TORI. I *KNOW* IT WAS YOU!!!

I'm still working on it.

guys in la

Like so many of us do after we've been dumped, I decided I could redeem myself by examining the choices I'd made and vowing to do the exact opposite from then on. I entered a classic phase of post-breakup overcorrection. This lasted about a year and came in two waves.

First, I became intensely wary of guys. I wasn't going to be made a fool of again. I once made plans with a sweet-faced bartender, and when he innocently asked to reschedule, I said, "You know, where I come from, this is called 'being blown off.'" *Where I come from*? Did I think I was from *The Dukes of Hazzard*?

Second, I wanted to exact my revenge on men in general. I realized that modern flirting was essentially just being mean while smiling. I hadn't mastered the whole getting people to like "the real me" thing, but insulting someone to their face? That I could do. And it seemed like the more attractive the guy was, the more he liked being insulted. We'd meet, I'd be charming (i.e., unnecessarily mean), we'd go on a few dates, I'd trick him into thinking he was in love with me, and then I'd stop returning his calls.

I wanted to punish someone for how I felt, but it never

helped. It was stupid and unwarranted. I guess I felt more in control for a while, but soon I realized I was no better than the cliché "geek" from high school who grows up and bones as many girls as possible out of spite. Which really took the fun out of it.

By twenty-two, I was back to business as usual love-wise: alternating between being contentedly alone and scaring off anyone I actually liked with my intensity and desperation. I did, however, implement a new rule: no discussion of "the number."

I'm happy to say that only a few years on, guys stopped thinking it was okay to ask me how many people I'd had sex with. I don't know if that change was a reflection of my age or the quality of men I was seeing, but there was a time when, if a guy had known me for more than twenty-four hours, he thought it was his right to know my complete sexual history.

This is a trap for girls. I always felt embarrassed about my late start in the sexual world, but the fiasco with Landon had taught me that you could be labeled slutty after having only one partner. Was my number too low or too high? And what did this information measure? An STI is an absolute; you either have one or you don't, and while a doctor can tell you that, knowing someone's number cannot.

Outside of a health concern, the question seemed designed only to shame and discourage promiscuity. And if that's the case, why just intercourse? Why did no one ask "How many people have touched your boobs?" or "How many penises have you seen?" or "Did you ever hump a swing set in first grade when no one was looking?" The logic is: I must avoid (even responsible, protected) sex with someone new, because it affects my "number," but this dude can go ahead and stick his face in my vagina because . . . who's counting? I decided that I would not engage with this ridiculous and arbitrary metric.*

The first time I implemented this new rule, I'd been seeing a guy for a couple weeks. He asked and I said something like, "I've decided to stop answering that question, because I think there is no answer that a woman can give without being judged. If it's a health matter, because you'd like to have sex with me, I can get tested and show you my results." I fully expected that when I said this, the guy might assume I'd had so many partners that I was embarrassed to reveal the number. But I figured if it weeds out the kind of guy who infers shame from reticence or thinks sexually active women are disgusting, all the better.

He took me up on the offer and we both got tested, which I respected. So far, so good! What I didn't count on was him pretending to be cool with me not answering while letting it fester and take on a life of its own. He brought it up several times in the following months. He never asked about my previous relationships, or my attitudes about sex or intimacy or fidelity. He wanted the number. I understood that if I simply told him that by his count he was number three, it would have brought him some comfort. But I didn't want to give it to him. He wanted

---

* Some dudes like to say that men have the instinct to spread their seed, while women are supposed to protect their reproductive organs from everything but the best sperm for the strongest potential offspring. By that logic every woman in the world should be saving herself for Dwayne "The Rock" Johnson and never let any of you shitheads touch her. Seriously, you guys should stop using that argument.

some assurance that I wasn't "too" experienced, but I didn't want to comfort someone who found that objectionable.

When we had our first big fight, his true colors came out. Slut. Whore. I'll bet you were molested when you were little. Charming, right? He was barking up the wrong tree in terms of trying to hurt me, but at least now I knew who I was dealing with.

In related news:

[INFOMERCIAL VOICE!]

Ladies, if you ever date a guy who shows up at your apartment uninvited, or calls you from someone else's phone when you block his number, or inspires you to attach a little can of Mace to your key ring, tell your friends! They will help you! If a guy threatens self-harm, or tells you that you are the crazy one and all your friends are on his side, they aren't! Your friends want to help you! And if you start talking yourself out of it because you're worried about looking overdramatic or vindictive because, I guess, he hasn't ever *hit* you . . . No! Don't do it! Don't talk yourself out of it! Your friends don't need you to get hit to want to help you! Yay!!!

Moving on.

Back on the Horse

More recently a friend of mine tried to play matchmaker for me. She proudly told me that the guy was reluctant to be set up until she showed him my picture. Of course, the picture she showed him was from a *GQ* shoot where I happened to be blond, backlit, and half naked. I texted her.

Me: Dude. Please get back to him and tell him to prepare to meet, like, a human woman. I did not know I would be attempting to live up to the expectation of a solid three man hours from a team of hair, makeup, and lighting professionals.

Sarah: Oh my god, stop, you're being ridiculous! ☺

Me: Let me do my impression of this guy's evening: "Oh, I don't know if I'm ready to meet anyone right now—wait! You didn't tell me she was a half-naked blonde with baby oil all over her legs! Let me Febreze my "going out" shirt and call an Uber!"

Me: Then "Aw, what's this? She's wearing clothes and isn't looking at me with lust in her eyes? I shaved my balls for nothing."

Me: Please tell him that since this photo was taken, I have dyed my hair back to its natural, mousy shade, and I have eaten several sandwiches.

He didn't show up.

I found that guys liked to showboat on the first few dates by talking restaurant managers into letting us in at closing time or hiking in restricted areas or sneaking into movies. These guys underestimated how much I love rules.

Also, while I love a good round of dirty talk, I don't enjoy bawdy talk. A lot of guys didn't understand that. For a while it seemed like men thought that pointing out that they had a penis would inspire some amazement on my part. I once told a guy I had to wake up early and he said, "I could wake you up with my—" Sir, I'll stop you right there.

That is the least sexy thing you could say to me. Nothing about you is sexy when you are the reason I am awake—you are basically an iPhone alarm with a pulse. And I don't want to fuck my iPhone. At least not at seven a.m.

But I get mine. For a while I had a fling with a guy who was so good-looking I think he was as confused by his interest in me as I was. The physical stuff was always great, but his perpetual expression was one of profound confusion. He obsessed over my body, but it seemed like it was because he was trying to locate the homing device that was scrambling his brain. I felt like saying, "I know, buddy, I don't get it, either. But . . . for now let's get you back to work!"

Something amazing happened to me when I hit my mid-twenties. I don't know how it happened—I didn't even notice it at first—but I stopped liking guys who didn't like me back. In fact, I stopped liking guys who were bad people. I wish I could impart some concrete advice about how to achieve this, because I have to tell you, it's incredible.

When I first realized this was happening I didn't want to mention it to anyone. I didn't even want to fully acknowledge it to myself. I thought I might jinx it or scare it away. How many times have I thought, *Wow, I guess I'm just at that point in my life where healthy foods are more appealing*, only to end up facedown in a plate of melted cheese and maple syrup.

I thought I was destined to fall for assholes forever. Misanthropic and fifteen years my senior? Sign me up! Makes misogynistic jokes but thinks I'm "feisty" for calling him on it? It's love! I'm still not certain I'm out of the woods—you never know where life will take you until you're awake at four a.m. dissecting text messages from a guy named Jordan who has a *The Wolf of Wall Street* poster in his bedroom.

But I think I might be done finding shallow and sad people attractive. It's paradise. *Pretty in Pink* was wrong; you can fall in love with Duckie.

A couple of years ago, I brought my boyfriend to a friend's weekly *Game of Thrones* viewing party. As the episode began and we all settled into our seats, two of the male attendees started whispering to each other.

"Oh my god, dude, you know who's on this show now? *Diana Rigg*. Wait 'til you see her." They seemed positively gleeful. These two grown men were giggling like bitchy cheerleaders at the fact that a woman who was once a sex symbol had the audacity to turn seventy-five and (gasp!) be on TV!! I reeled from witnessing this exchange, and as I prepared to ask just what the hell that was supposed to mean, my boyfriend chimed in.

"Oh, Diana Rigg, man! She's been on the last few episodes; she's brilliant in this, right?" My sweet boyfriend didn't even notice when the two men shot each other smug "That's not what we meant, buddy" glances.

When we left I told him, "You realize what you've done, right? You just expressed that it's possible for a woman you don't find sexually attractive to have value. I think those guys might think less of you now."

"Really? I hate those guys. So that would be great."

● ● ●

I've still got stuff to work on. If a guy can convince me he has the answers or a better plan than me, I will follow him anywhere. I've fallen for it more than once. It's not easy to pull off, because I happen to think most people are idiots, but if you can do it, I'm in trouble.

I would follow a confident woman just as blindly. However, in my experience, women are less comfortable pretending to know what they're doing when they don't.

I've been on the other side of it, too. I've met the guy who is young and talented and wise beyond his years and still looks to me for advice. What an ego trip that is. It took an older man saying point-blank "I like giving you advice" for me to realize that yes, that's the bit you like. Not being helpful to me, but the sound of your authority reverberating in the ears of a younger woman.

It's not that deep down I want someone to "take care of me," it's that I'm exhausted, and occasionally overwhelmed by self-doubt. I'm steering the ship, but I don't know what I'm doing. None of us do. But it would be *so nice* to believe that someone out there did, and that maybe they could take the wheel for a little while.

It's a seductive feeling. It would be great if it were real. But I guess I've got to count on myself. Which is not great news.

Hollywood

fashion

Suit Up

In third grade my fashion hero was Claudia from the Baby-Sitters Club books. She was into fashion and junk food and art and being Japanese. I was into the first two things, so I figured I could model myself after her. I used to reread every description of her outfits (usually found in chapter two, where the POV character describes the other club members), and I compiled them all in a notebook. When my family went to the mall I'd stay on the lookout for things like purple high-tops and printed turtlenecks. Unfortunately, the books were written in the mid-eighties and it was 1993, so my fashion hero was pretty "five minutes ago" but would be right on point today. What's that? The mid-eighties are out again? AND the mid-nineties are out? 2002 is in? Wasn't that like three years ago??

Since I could never find what I needed to precisely re-create Claudia's every outfit, I settled for coveting the most absurd-looking articles of clothing at Contempo Casuals or T.J. Maxx. I was eight years old at this point, and my mother had a brilliant plan: occasionally buy me a stupid-looking outfit, let me wear it, and I'd get it out of my system before I got to high school.

For the most part, "stupid-looking" was the worst offense: stretch pants with sequined piping from my brother's Michael Jackson Halloween costume, a sweatshirt with an iron-on appliqué and puff paint, a massive faux mother-of-pearl daisy necklace—ya know, stupid-looking. Some of it, though, was hilariously "provocative." My favorite piece was a black halter top that tied in the back and around the neck. Over it, I wore a sheer white collared shirt with black velvet polka dots, tied up at the bottom. I looked dope. I think I even wore it in our class picture. On its intended customer, this halter top probably would have shown off the navel and full abs as well as a generous helping of cleavage. On me (the eight-year-old fetus) it covered my entire torso, almost up to my neck. It was the equivalent to a toddler wearing an actual dress Paris Hilton got up-skirted in—they'd smell like a stripper but they'd look like a nun.

It caused something of a stir among the other parents. They'd chirp to my mother, "Wow, you let your daughter wear a halter top to school?"

"Yeah, why not, right? If I tell her what to wear now, she'll just want to rebel even more when she's sixteen."

"Oooh, what a neat idea. Not for me, though, I could never let my kid dress like that."

"Okay, but ten bucks says she's gonna start dressing like a tramp the second she gets boobs." Mom would actually wait and say that to me in the car, but it was still awesome.

Even at eight I knew it was pretty pathetic for someone else's parents to care about what I wore. Perhaps it should have prepared me for my current state of affairs, where my clothing is the subject of professional debate for equally unaffected people. Bring on the critique, *Fashion Police*! My mom's gonna have a wicked burn all lined up the second you turn your back!

When I got to middle school my style was informed by the rise of two movements: grunge (which had finally hit Maine) and my personal self-loathing. Even in the summer I wore long sleeves, because a schoolmate gently pointed out that the hair on my arms was dark and revolting. It's gone away now after years of waxing and perhaps sheer force of will. If you still have dark hair on your arms maybe you don't hate yourself enough. My mom told me that she had dark hair on her arms as a kid, but it went away as she grew up and the same thing would probably happen to me. (That doesn't help me right now, idiot! I'm an abomination!!!) I made sure to find clothing that covered as much real estate as possible.

For the most part I had to shop in the kids' sections of JC Penney and L.L.Bean, but large children's sizes kept me plenty covered. There was an especially unfortunate plaid bucket hat, and a daisy-covered wallet with . . . a chain. The memory of this wallet chain pops up whenever I've been feeling too good about myself. I mostly used clothes as a means to avoid detection. It's like I thought that if my shirts were baggy enough, I'd be mistaken for a pile of laundry that moved from class to class.

In high school, clothing became armor. Other girls dressed to accentuate whatever they were working with. Since I was working with nothing, I relied on my flared corduroys and a revolving collection of lewd T-shirts. Now, some of you will have to trust me on this, but there was a time before every douche bag had a "Jesus Is My Homeboy" shirt when printed tees were an actual novelty, especially to Mainers. Around fourteen, I discovered a store called Yellow Rat Bastard. (Shut up! That store used to be cool!) Every time I went to New York for an audition, I'd find my way to Prince Street and buy a funny and occasionally obscene T-shirt.

The shirts were always too big for me, so they hid the fact that I had the measurements of a hairless cat, and they were rude, so they gave off a real "I could dress in cute clothes if I wanted but I'm above it" vibe. One had a picture of Pee-wee Herman captioned "Pervert." Another had the cast of *Baywatch* and the word "ORGY." I layered them over long-sleeve waffle tees and took on the world. *I can't feel bad that I'm not one of the pretty girls if I'm actively making myself look weird! Loophole!* I wanted to be sent home for my inappropriate clothing. Badly. True to form, though, I was terrified and filled with regret the only time a teacher mentioned it.

When Abercrombie & Fitch came to the Maine Mall and created a scramble among the wealthier kids to prove they could afford it, I shoplifted a shirt and wrote "Am I Popular Yet" across the chest with a marker. Suck it, fashion! I'm not your bitch!

Sometime during junior year my friend Sam told me that when guys walked into a room, they scanned the girls and picked out who they'd have sex with. He explained that it was like a reflex, so I'd love to get some feedback from guys on whether this is true. Just tweet me or leave an Instagram comment, or if you see me in the grocery store definitely just come up and let me know. When I asked if I made his list, he shrugged and said, "Yeah, you're always on the 'I would' side. I think you're probably on most guys' 'I would' side."

This. Was. Great. News. Given the choice, with no effort required, guys would rather have sex with me than not have sex with me? This changed everything! I mean, I still didn't want to have sex, but you're saying that if I DID I wouldn't have to promise to wash the guy's car to get him on board? The revelation that in spite of my boy-chest and braces I wasn't considered a monstrosity led to about eight months of really sad attempts to highlight my AA cups and gel (gel!) my hair into submission. Turns out that trying to look as pretty as you can and still not being a pretty girl does a real number on you. My waffle tees were more comfortable anyway.

Audition Closet

Reverting back to my homely-by-choice tactic served me well when I moved to Los Angeles. I'd never seen people this good-looking. I know lots of people say that LA is full of tall blondes who make you feel like Quasimodo's ugly cousin. I know it's unoriginal and feels like a cry for attention. But when you're auditioning to say one line on an episode of *Entourage*, you can't help but think, *Even I would cast this part on looks alone*, then scan the room and regret using your last quarter for street parking.

Maybe I had to compete with these girls at auditions, but I was not about to battle the changing tides of style in my spare time. Boho chic is in, you say? Cool, I'm gonna go buy a *Sponge-Bob* jacket from the boys' section of Target.

My closet looked like the by-product of schizophrenia. When you're searching for an acting job, you never throw anything away because, you know, what if there's an audition for a futuristic businesswoman who happened to spill ketchup on herself earlier that day? And if something is cheap enough, you'll buy even the most hideous garments for the same reason. Your personal clothing is less than half of what you own. And no matter how strong you are, you will end up wearing something regrettable like your "spoiled homecoming queen" audition outfit to a party and take a photo with your friend Lacy where you're both obviously sucking in your stomachs. Maybe your photos will be higher than three megapixels, but it will happen.

For the most part, though, I was happy with my sartorial choices. I thought I looked cool. Maybe I did. Or maybe I looked homeless. Either way, it didn't occur to me that adults who weren't auditioning or on a date could wear decent clothes. I once went to dinner with Aubrey Plaza and when she showed up in a skirt and a little white blazer, I thought, *Is she going somewhere after this?*

Enter the Stylist

The *Twilight* premiere was my first experience with a stylist. Actually, he was more a friend of a friend who told me he could convince some less-reputable showrooms that he was a stylist, but he was willing to work for free, so the job was his! He got me three dresses: the pink one was too small, the silver one made me look like the world's saddest sex robot, and the black one . . . sort of fit. We decided on the black one.

After the premiere, a costume designer friend told me he'd seen a picture of me in a magazine. "You looked cute, you were wearing this kind of kooky black dress." Kooky? "Yeah, it had a ruffle around the collar and a kind of kooky bell sleeve." It had a ruffle around the collar? It had sleeves? All I had noticed was that it was a black dress. And it fit me. And it didn't make me look like C-3PO's slave wife. I had thought of it as the "safe" option, as a "little black dress." Turns out someone who knew stuff about clothes immediately identified it as "eccentric." Lucky for me, he seemed charmed by it. I'd gotten away with "taking a risk" on my first real red carpet. Also, I was the thirty-seventh-most-important character in the Twilight movies, so no one gave a shit anyway.

When *Up in the Air* was chosen to premiere at the Toronto International Film Festival, Paramount Pictures hired a professional stylist for me. I suspect word had gotten back to them that I enjoyed dressing like a teenager who lived in her car, and while that was spectacularly endearing, it would be in their best interest to have someone help me dress like an adult woman. I wanted to do whatever I was supposed to do to promote a movie of that caliber, and I was excited about the prospect of playing dress-up in free clothes instead of begrudgingly spending money I needed for Panda Express at Bebe whenever I got invited to something.

Since the movie wasn't out yet, and to fashion people indie

films don't "count," my stylist was effectively working with someone who had no credits. To be honest, I don't understand how styling works to this day and I've given up trying to figure it out. I think part of the ambiguity comes from the stylist wanting to protect you from the harsh realities of the fashion world. If I mention in an email that I think some designer makes especially beautiful dresses, and my stylist never gets back to me about it, I can assume she didn't want to say, "No, honey, that designer is a huge deal and you've been in one movie that hasn't come out yet." So you both pretend the email never happened.

The first time I went to my stylist's house and pawed through a rack of dresses, it felt like Christmas. When I tried them all on, it felt more like Christmas without presents, food, or alcohol. Her distinctly unfamous client was not a big selling point for designers to give up their best stuff. You can only try on so many olive-green paisley numbers before you seriously consider creating a dress from toilet paper and bedsheets. But buried in this mountain of lamé and brocade, there was one gorgeous soft-pink Marchesa. I still don't know how she got it. I don't know if the dress was lined with asbestos, or if they owed her a favor, or if she stole it out of a pile reserved for Anne Hathaway. I had no credits but we got a Marchesa. And the fucker fit. (Also, I learned that things which I thought fit didn't fit. "Fit" to me now means: it looks more like a piece of clothing than a garbage bag, and it can be made to "fit" with extensive tailoring.)

We decided to go with the pink dress, and after we got it tailored and found a bra that didn't show, my stylist asked me about shoes. She thought it was important that I wear a pair of expensive shoes—not just dressy-looking shoes, actual expensive shoes. It turned out magazines were going to decide how seriously to take me based on whether I wore designer shoes or shoes that *looked* nice but didn't cost enough to feed a family for a month, like some kind of phony. She came to my apartment with three pairs of shoes in a shopping bag and said we should pick one pair and she'd return the rest.

"The Louboutins are a little pricier than the others, but it's your first big premiere, and I think they're really special."

"Okay, how much are those?"

"One thousand ninety-nine."

Dollars? A thousand dollars?! That's more than my rent! Like, a lot more! Maybe you've noticed that I live with two dudes and sleep in an Ikea twin bed. Or has living in a world of luxury for so long left you unable to recognize the signature lines and craftsmanship of the Malm collection? (For context: my stylist was earning more to dress me for *Up in the Air*–related events than I did for making the actual movie.) There was a feeling from the people around me at that time that although I hadn't made much money yet, things were about to start going so well that huge checks were right around the corner! I should spend whatever I had to, even if it seemed imprudent, because I'd have tons of money in just a few months! I'm glad I was such a tightfisted bitch, because the money didn't follow for about two years. In fact, *Twilight* was the only thing keeping me above water. I've said in the past that without that series I would have been evicted, and people think I'm joking. Nope. Me and my Oscar nom would have been living in my car. Which is a charming story now, but at the time, I did not find it funny.

The shoe situation, though, seemed like a necessary evil. Apparently, I was now trying to convince the world that I was a movie star, and movie stars had companies like Louboutin *begging* them to wear their shoes! And to pretend that that was happening, I would have to buy a pair. I paid a thousand dollars to trick people into thinking I got free shoes.

I wore the shoes in Toronto with my awesome and inexplicable Marchesa dress. No one seemed to care one way or the other about what was on my feet, but maybe it's one of those "you only notice it if it's Aldo" kind of things. I still have those shoes. I don't think I've worn them since. If they go out of style, or I join a cult that eschews material goods, or if both my feet are eaten off by the army of cats I'll eventually own, I'll never get rid of those shoes. Yes, it's the ultimate irony that I can now afford a pair of shoes like that, but designers let me borrow them for free. When you think about it, all these celebrities are borrowing shoes that have been worn by someone else before them. Like bowling shoes. So the joke's on us.

Yep. Two inanimate objects. Truly the stuff of nightmares.

That story makes my stylist sound crazy, which she wasn't; she was just used to the fashion world. I'd encountered this behavior before when I did a photo shoot for *Teen Vogue* with the cast of *Rocket Science*. I loved the shoes they put me in, and the magazine's stylist said, "Oh, they're actually from that designer's diffusion line, so they're not that expensive—I think they're like six or seven hundred." Cool. That's when I started cutting the labels out of the clothes I wore to fashion shoots, lest they see an Old Navy tag as I undress and kick me out of their studio.

A Good Sport

A few nights before the Oscars I was invited to a party thrown by Louis Vuitton. When a fashion house throws a party, they send clothing options to the invitees so that no one shows up in Chanel and rips apart the space-time continuum. My stylist was beaming as she showed me a beautiful white coat and a pleated tartan minidress. I put it on and immediately said, "Oh my god, it's like a high-end slutty schoolgirl costume. It's fucking amazing." It was weird but it was cool and I liked it. I looked like a luxury tramp and it was a nice change of pace from what I'd been wearing during all the Oscars press. When I got to the party and started to take off my coat, the woman next to me looked at my dress and said, "Is that what they sent you to wear? Aw. You're a good sport."

I put down my drink; I needed both hands to tie my coat back up tight enough that it wouldn't show a square centimeter of my dress. I spent the rest of the night readjusting my collar higher on my neck, and only when the house photographer stopped me in the hallway on my way out did I take the coat off, praying that no one would pass by.

All the photos that ran in fashionland the next day were of me in a voluminous white coat. I met with my stylist to look at Oscar dresses and said, "Oh man, you won't believe what I did last night."

"No, I saw." She was a little terse.

"Right . . . It's just that this woman, like, said I was a 'good sport' for wearing the dress, and it felt like a dig and—"

"She said that? She saw what you were wearing and felt moved to say something passive-aggressive to you?"

"Yeah, basically."

"Wow," she said with a smirk. "She felt so provoked by a fucking *dress* that she took a swipe at you. That's pathetic. Man, if you're messing up someone's day with what you're wearing, you're doing something right."

I liked that. That even someone from the fashion world was like, *Dude, it's just fashion. It's supposed to be fun.*

No one had prepared me for this part. I didn't know I was going to have to learn about fashion. I thought I knew plenty about fashion. I knew gowns were more formal than short dresses, skirts were more formal than pants, and leaving the house in just socks and a sports bra would get you arrested. Now you're telling me there's more to fashion than finding a dress that shows enough boob to distract from your face?

I struggle with fashion, because growing up the way I did, it felt like something explicitly designed to distinguish people with money from people like me. Reading a magazine that said I was "supposed to" have some new bag or dress I couldn't afford felt like crap. Now I get to wear these beautiful dresses and it's hard to reconcile.

The first time I went to a fashion show, I went backstage afterward to meet the designer. I expected her to tell me the dress was really intended for someone less pasty and walk away. But she was nervous. She was almost beside herself. She was asking me what I thought of the show and telling me she wasn't going to read reviews until the next day so that no matter what, she could at least enjoy the fruits of her labor for the rest of the night. She'd studied and worked for years; she'd crafted the pieces meticulously with the best materials and construction. This was her art, and I was looking at it like a corporate conspiracy to make me feel insecure.

Fashion is an art form and an expression of self. Creative outlets are hard to find, and if fashion is yours, go deep with it, baby; I can't wait to see you shine. But if you're feeling crappy because you accidentally scrolled through Gigi Hadid's Instagram, remember, it's just fashion. It's supposed to be fun.

Now, going to events that are important to me or to colleagues is part of my life. I'm grateful to have anything to celebrate in my world, and if current custom dictates that I look halfway decent, I don't want to disrespect that. I want to honor the event that I'm at and the designer who allows me to wear their work. I'm glad I got to see the vulnerable person behind an intimidating fashion show. I'm also grateful that someone shook me out of my protective shell of self-righteousness. It's healthy.

Even though I like my shell very much. There will always be people who use fashion as a status symbol. But I don't wanna be friends with those people anyway.

Oh, Honey

Now I know just enough to know that I don't know anything.

I learned there's something called bias cut, which means that it's going to look terrible on you unless you're Gisele. I learned that nude shoes make your legs look longer. And I learned that before going out you should shine a very bright light at your crotch to make sure you can't see your puss.

Short girls: get it tailored. For GOD'S SAKE, get it tailored! The wardrobe designer on *Pitch Perfect*, Sal Pérez, hammered this home for me because we don't wear business clothes or silk dresses in those films, we wear T-shirts and denim jackets, and still, alterations are made. I used to just deal with the extra fabric that bunched at the bottom of my jeans until Sal had me try on a pair of Rag & Bone. I flew out of the dressing room. "This is amazing! It fits so well, even in the inseam!" I admired myself in the mirror, then sheepishly asked, "Does it fit because it's a 'cigarette' cut?" Sal put his hand on my shoulder. "Oh, honey, it's a capri." So, non-capri pants might need hemming, but it's totally worth it. Just because it's not a luxury item doesn't mean you're a jerk for getting it altered.

Also, take in the sleeve! That's the BEST trick I've learned for getting tops and jackets to look right on us shorties. Don't just take the sleeve up at the wrist, take IN the width of the sleeve.

It's a game changer. The same is true of men's suits. Men, even more so than women, seem to think that getting something to look "good" is about going up in price, but tell your boyfriend to get a less expensive suit and have it tailored. Please, as a service to me.

Wear the Spanx. You might not want to squeeze them over your ass in the morning, but when you see that mac and cheese at lunch (do it, you beautiful monster) you'll be glad they're there, doing the lord's work.

Never, ever, even if she is on the brink of hypothermia, let your taller, blonder friend borrow your favorite pea coat. You look good in that coat. But she will look better. And you'll never be able to unsee it. (This is not based on me, or a Topshop coat, or my friend Lea.)

If you want "real" fashion advice, you should look up Alexa Chung or Olivia Palermo, who, while they are good at lots of other stuff, are known for wearing clothes really well. I would argue that the most honest fashion advice they could give would be, "Be tall, thin, and gorgeous, and have a monthly budget of around five hundred dollars for maintaining your hair," but if you look them up I'm sure that every interviewer has asked them, "What's your best fashion advice?" and they have answered, "Wear what makes you feel confident." By the way, who has that helped? What girl is out there thinking, *Dammit, I've been wearing my least-favorite articles of clothing, because I thought you were supposed to feel dumpy and shy. Clothes AREN'T supposed to make you want to avoid human contact? Thank you, Olivia Palermo, thank you.* (I'm just being shitty; it's a lame question because there's no good answer. These girls have their QUOTE™ down and they stick to it. Keep climbin', ladies.)

Sidebar: The only reason I feel bad about bringing them up is that at some point Alexa and Olivia will be asked on some red carpet, "What do you think of Anna Kendrick's burn in her book?" and they'll have to go, "Who?" and then their publicist will tell them and they will have to say something like, "Oh, she's entitled to her opinion," or "She's obviously just kidding," or hopefully "What a cunt," and then the fun REALLY begins.

I'm trying to have fun. I get to wear fancy clothes and I get to have my hair and makeup done, and being a little brat about it is stupid. I also *have* to wear fancy clothes and have my hair and makeup done. And anything in the world that you *have* to do can become tiresome. If you had to play with a puppy every day—okay, that's not a good example; that would always be fun. But someone poking your eye with a makeup brush is not as fun as a puppy; you'll just have to take my word for it.

making movies is a fool's errand

I need a lot of sleep. More sleep than I'd like. I wish I could be one of those people who thrives on five hours a night, but I really need seven or eight—just to function. I'll happily take nine. Ten, if you're offering. I'm actually gonna lie down for a minute.

Okay, that was nice. Maybe I need more iron in my diet. I bring it up because on a film set, sleep becomes the ultimate commodity. The hours are fucking bananas. We're certainly not curing cancer, but man do we stay at work like we're trying.

Portrait of a professional with energy drink, 4 a.m.

All you do when you're making a movie is sleep and go to work. You're staying in a hotel or a rented apartment, miles and often several time zones away from anyone you know. It's hard to see outside the little world you're in. You can't get perspective because for the duration of the shoot, nothing else exists. So you are at the mercy of the people around you. The group you are working with (a.k.a. your only waking companions) will dictate whether you are going to spend a few months euphoric or miserable.

Sometimes it's awesome. When you know there's a ticking clock on your relationships, it's fun to get way too close way too fast. Why pace yourself? You won't even have time to get sick of each other! You jump into intense friendships and it's bittersweet and wonderful. Sometimes you don't like the people you're working with. It's temporary, but facing another sixteen-hour block with people you don't like can feel insurmountable even when you know it's only for a few months. Getting on Skype with your best friend to talk shit helps, but you gotta go to sleep and do it all over again in six hours, so make your shit talk count!

I try not to let it, but my personal feelings can affect how I approach filming. I once got into a debate with a director because I didn't understand why I would kiss the actor in the scene with me. I felt like there was simply *no* motivation for them to kiss in that moment. The director pointed out that we were playing boyfriend and girlfriend and couples tend to . . . kiss. Oh, right! So we kissed. But I wasn't *happy* about it!

It's also hard to gauge how well a scene is working if you don't get along with someone in it. Once you know someone is an asshole, it's hard to find anything they say funny, charming, or poignant. I find myself thinking, *I wouldn't believe this guy if he warned me about an impending nuclear fallout; he's an asshole.*

Sometimes, though, nothing bonds a cast like a common enemy. For an independent film I once did, an acting coach was hired. I've never been sure why; it's certainly not common practice. She took herself very seriously, so we felt we had to take her seriously as well. We did an exercise in pairs where we ran across a room toward each other and jumped as high as we could at the point of intersection. After a while, my woefully unathletic ass said, "Hey, I'm sort of out of breath here, can I take a break for a second?"

"No, keep going. Jump higher."

Um, are you my Soviet gymnastics coach? I thought we were all adults, and I thought we all kind of understood that this "acting exercise" was New Age bullshit.

I prepared to run at my partner.

Fuck me, now I've got to commit twice as hard or she might make me keep doing it.

But that's the trouble with being an anemic little weakling: you can't just draw from your reserve of energy and focus, because you don't have one.

It was immediately clear that I wasn't going to improve, so she had me do enough runs to conceivably be satisfied and said, "That was great work. Much better, Anna."

We thanked her for all her help and left. That night the whole cast went to dinner and one of the men was the first to break.

"Okay, that lady was crazy, right?"

The rest of us couldn't agree fast enough. I ended up feeling closer to that cast than most others. If I ever direct something I'm going to hire one crazy person so that everyone else gets along.

Film sets are unpredictable; it's like trying to put together a wedding every day, in the middle of an uncharted forest. (Sometimes literally. More on that later.) There's an expression about how you can account for everything, dot your i's and cross your t's, be totally prepared . . . then an elephant escapes from the zoo and runs through your set. I was shooting a movie in a tiny town in Indiana. I mean tiny, like "stables in the Walmart parking lot for the Amish residents" tiny. It should have been ideal for shooting, because there would be no interruptions. Once we started filming, though, we noticed something. Trains came through the neighboring town about every ten minutes. No one had heard the sound before, because in the whole time they were scouting locations they'd never stood perfectly still and quiet in a room for ten minutes. Unfortunately, that's all you do on a film set. The flat landscape and paucity of residents ensured that the sound carried perfectly. About two thirds of everything we shot was unusable.

Making movies is a fool's errand. It's madness. And there's never a guarantee that it will work. And yet, people keep coming back. Businesspeople who are smart enough to know better keep investing in movies. Kids keep going to film school. M. Night Shyamalan can't be stopped. And for some reason, neither can I.

Nudity

Nudity really isn't for me. Why? Eh . . . I've tried explaining it to people, but it seems you either immediately understand, or you don't see what the big deal is. I don't mind a *sex* scene. A *character* can be having a sex scene, but my physical parts always feel like mine. 'Cause . . . they are. See, it's hard to put into words. I don't object at all to the use of nudity in film; it can add realism and intimacy. And by the way, more power to the actors who are comfortable with it, but for the time being, it's not for me.

I did once get to choose my own butt double (for a scene where so little of "my butt" showed that I doubt anyone really noticed that it happened). Having never done it before, I was relieved to find out the selection process is not done in person. Instead, I was handed a black binder to look through. Inside was a small collection of Polaroids. Naked girls against a white wall, shot from the neck down. It looked like something out of *The Silence of the Lambs*.

First of all, I didn't know why they'd been photographed from the front at all; I was only looking for a butt double, and the frontal pics just made me feel like an even bigger creep. (I still looked, though.) And second, as I perused my butt options, I realized I didn't know what my own butt looked like. It's behind me all the time, and even when I've looked at it in a mirror I'm usually twisting my body around to see if that tender spot is a pimple or if I sat on a thumbtack.

I inspected the selection of anonymous bottoms, and just as I was about to say, "I think this girl looks like me?" the (female) producer casually pointed to my impending choice and said, "Well, this one's butt is a little square. I think we can rule her out." What? Is that a thing? I didn't know a butt could be square. Do *I* have a square butt? You know what? Don't tell me.

Kissing

I do not find kissing scenes fun at all. I had assumed that was the lie actors had to stick to because admitting it was awesome would make them seem creepy or piss off their spouses. There's always talk of how "people are standing around" and "it's awkward" and "you're doing it over and over," but that didn't seem like enough to negate the awesome to me.

I always thought that if I got to do kissing scenes I'd toe the party line but deep down I'd be thinking, *We basically get to cheat here without getting in trouble, so . . . it's kind of great.* And I've heard that some people do think it's great! So bully for them—I'm envious!—but I find it totally clinical. It's not about the people standing around, it's about the fact that the other person doesn't *want* to be kissing you. They are obligated to do it. They might not be horrified, but it wasn't their decision.

I could try saying, "Hey, um, is there any chance that you're, like, secretly into me? Because if you were it would make this work assignment we're about to do way more fun for me." But that doesn't seem super professional. Most of the time I don't even remember anything about it.

I have been excited about kissing a costar precisely one time. One time! And it wasn't even until after the fact! I won't name names since I don't want to embarrass him, but let me recount this tale quickly.

A couple of years ago I did a small role in an improvised film as a favor to a friend. I had a short scene with a handsome movie star. Our movie backstory was that we'd had a fling in the past, we were friendly now, and it was all a little flirtatious, but we weren't serious about each other. There was no plan to kiss, just some light chat. As for my real-life backstory, I'd had a crush on this actor as a teenager, so maybe I should have been nervous and excited to work with him, BUT my character had to give him stitches. On his face. On his handsome movie-star face. I needed to concentrate on not drawing blood at any point. The only thing that stood between his face and the very sharp, very real needle in my hand was a layer of latex prosthetic, as thin as fresh prosciutto. I also knew that he was the kind of committed actor who wouldn't stop a scene to say, "Ow. That's my actual face you're ripping into, so hey, maybe we should cut."

Halfway through the evening, I still hadn't permanently scarred any coworkers, and as we got more comfortable with the scene, the director leaned in and said, "It felt like you guys were going to kiss in that last take. I think it was a good instinct, maybe we should go with that."

Okay. We each got a mint, and for a few takes we stumbled through the double awkwardness that is kissing onscreen without an exact cue to do it.

At the end of the night, I went home happy with the work we'd done and relieved that no flesh was harmed. I drove all the way home, pulled into my driveway, and, as I was putting the car in park, suddenly *shrieked*, "Oh my god, I just made out with Legolas!"

Again, I'm not going to name that actor, as I wish to respect his privacy.

Budget

Into the Woods was one of the biggest-budget films I've ever worked on. It made the production glorious. Every single detail in that film was designed with love and passion. The world created by Rob Marshall and his team was so rich, I felt inspired and grateful on a daily basis in a way that is VERY unusual for me. A larger budget enables a fully realized vision, but it inspires overcomplicated solutions to nonproblems. It also has some comical side effects.

There's a scene in *Into the Woods* where Cinderella runs down the palace stairs, but Prince Charming has covered them in sticky tar to keep her from getting away. As that scene approached, someone asked me to try on my "magnet shoes." "My what?" No one had bothered to ask me, but some mystery higher-up had assumed that I wouldn't be able to "stop in my tracks" unassisted and tasked several departments with fitting both the stairs and *my shoes* with powerful electromagnets. The idea was to switch them on as I ran full speed down concrete steps.

Now, this was not only a spectacular waste of time and resources, it was kind of a fucking death trap. Even if it worked, I would surely be sent flying out of the shoes and into some corrective surgery. I had to do a couple of runs to prove to Rob that

I could successfully mime being stuck in goo, and I let the special effects guys turn on the magnets when Cinderella struggles to pry her shoes up by hand, so that everyone could feel like Operation Electro-Murder had been a justifiable project.

My second-favorite thing about that scene was that Chris Pine, who played the prince, had to stand there THE WHOLE TIME. Both of us assumed he'd come in for an hour in the morning, they'd shoot some footage, and through movie magic, he would appear frozen in time at the top of the stairs. No such luck. Poor Chris had to stand there and watch me do that number a hundred times. I was running, crawling, falling down, jumping up, and belting my stupid face off for two days straight, and with every "action" he trudged back into position and endured another take.

I'll admit I found the situation amusing. Every time he complained it just gave me an easy opening to say, "Oh, I'm so sorry that YOU had to work hard today. Can somebody get Chris a medal?"

Here's the thing: I really felt for him. A long day at work is made abnormally grueling by an absence of productivity or accomplishment. For all the physical and mental energy I was expending (and the bruises I was getting), I left those two days so content and satisfied. He left them needing a burger just to get a little dopamine flowing in his brain before we had to start all over again.

There were also two small fires on set that no one seemed to be that worried about. I do mean small, but still. A scrim and a prop lantern (which was not built for actual flames) caught on fire, and there was no real sense of hustle. This was a big-budget film; there was a department for that. This is how a roomful of adults ends up staring at a rapidly growing fire with their mouths open.

The previous year, I'd been shooting the movie *Happy Christmas* with a total of six crew members and about four principal actors. If there'd been a fire, all ten of us would have run to a water source. (Unless it was a grease fire; we're filmmakers, not idiots.*)

When you're on an independent film, you have to wear more hats. It isn't stressful, though, because you start to feel capable and relish the responsibility. *Happy Christmas* was shot in eleven days for eighty thousand dollars (for perspective, that's 1/262nd the budget of *Silver Linings Playbook*). There was no script, no paper involved whatsoever. And we didn't tell anyone we were doing it.

Aspiring filmmakers: Isn't it great news that you can make a movie for so little, and, more important, that you don't need to ask permission? It was the happiest and most productive set I've ever been on. I'm not saying small-scale movies are always better off on the whole—I don't want the next Bond film to be improvised and shot handheld. You can't make a movie about an alien-werewolf invasion with ten people and eighty grand. And I want to see *Fur from the Sky* by 2018.

---

* Debatable.

Wardrobe

I've wanted to work on a period piece for as long as I can remember. A fantasy period piece even more so. I got my wish with *Into the Woods*, and it was everything I dreamed it could be. And a little less. Turns out, authentically made corsets are quite small. They seemed bearable in my fitting, but any woman who's ever tried on shoes in a store knows that you can think something is perfectly comfortable only to wind up begging for mercy at the end of your first day in them.

In between scenes, I could ask to have my corset loosened and get some relief (I couldn't do it myself because of how it was made), but inevitably, it had to get laced up again. This led to an unusual dynamic between Asia, the on-set dresser, and me. I adored Asia. She was funny, hardworking, and sweet. But she was responsible for putting me in a moderate degree of physical distress. If your best friend gave you a charley horse ten times a day, you'd feel weird about her, too. So after a few weeks, whenever I saw Asia (Lovely Asia! Whom I really liked!) it struck fear into my heart. We would eye each other across the set, awaiting the telltale signs of camera readiness. This equally tiny blonde and I would get locked in a stare-down like bull and matador. Eventually, I'd lose focus and Asia would creep up behind me.

"Oh, hi, Asia, are we sure they're ready? I thought we were waiting on the animal wrangler to bring the cow?" I said, stalling.

"Nope"—tug, tug, tug—"the cow's already set." Tug, tug, tug. "Dion's just swinging a lens and then picture's up."

I'd get desperate. "Oh"—tug, tug, tug—"I feel like the cow always runs away a couple times before we actually shoot, though, so maybe just a few more minutes—"

But she was the matador, and she skewered me every time.

Our legendary costume designer, Colleen Atwood, had every piece that we wore custom-made, and she handpicked the perfect fabrics, laces, and buttons. Even the shoes were made by hand. The skirt on Cinderella's "rags" was a dusty-blue linen. It was humble but lovely—the perfect choice for Cinders—but linen is a fabric that wrinkles like Jack Nicholson's balls without Botox.

So I'm working in a corset and heels for sixteen-hour days, but every single time I sit—just sit down and have a little rest in between takes—someone has to steam my skirt, because it now has some minor wrinkles in it. I'm *Cinderella*, by the way. My body, my hair, every part of my costume has been painstakingly covered in soot and grime and grass. God forbid my skirt isn't freshly pressed.

The most annoying part was that Colleen was right; it really did look better smooth. Dirty and disheveled added to the aesthetic, but wrinkled was distracting. It was this major production, Disney's Christmas tentpole, and I couldn't even sit down. So in between takes I'd walk over to a chair or a bench and just look at it. Longingly. Sometimes I'd lean on it. Or circle it like a cat. People on that set probably thought I had hemorrhoids.

My wardrobe on *Up in the Air* was perfectly curated for my character. But it felt so unnatural to me, as did the rest of my look—the hair and the makeup—that I started to feel claustrophobic in it as the weeks went on. I bought some glittery nail polish in an alarming shade of blue and painted my toes so that I could be in control of one small corner of my body. Natalie would never wear something so juvenile, but I liked knowing that under my perfectly tailored skirt suit, I was still messy and strange.

My tiny act of rebellion was discovered on the day we shot a scene at airport security. I had counted on Natalie always wearing closed-toed shoes, but even in movie-land, the TSA is unflinchingly scrupulous. I pulled at the toes of my nude stockings until enough material gathered to obscure my sparkling nails. Our costume designer, Danny Glicker, as acerbic as he is brilliant, looked me up and down and raised his eyebrow. *Your secret's safe with me, but that's an unfortunate look.* No one else on set seemed to notice. That scene was cut anyway. Perhaps test audiences were thrown by how guilty Natalie looked during a simple airport security check.

Keeping Up Appearances

When you start a new film, you come to work looking nice for the first week. Then, inevitably, you remember that you are in your personal clothes for thirty minutes each morning and your costume for the next fifteen hours. All right! Same pair of sweatpants every day for a month, here I come! By week three, if an actor is still coming to work in a full outfit at four a.m., you can be sure that they're banging someone on set.

The same is true for your appearance from the neck up. You show up looking like hell on toast and, lucky for you, some poor sap has to put your face and hair into some recognizably human arrangement before the first shot.

I've been told I have "working-girl hair." I like this expression because it sounds like my hair is a swarthy, streetwise prostitute in 1930s New York. It's actually a reference to the damage your hair goes through when you are on a film set. The more movies you make, the worse the damage from blow-drying, curling, coloring, etc. In this sense the term is supposed to be worn as a badge of honor, a testament to your work ethic—like calling your dark under-eye bags "success circles" or "ambition sacs." What it actually means is that your hair is wiry and brittle with thin ends, and will need even more blow-drying, curling, and coloring to be made camera-ready.

I had very curly hair when I was growing up, but I WILLED IT AWAY and now my hair dries naturally into gentle waves. (I heat-style my hair every single day so I don't look like Dale Dickey in *Winter's Bone*.) I used Frizz Ease for years until my first on-set hairstylist pointed out that the frizzy "before" picture was just a straight-haired model who'd been photographed with "messy" hair through some contrivance. I'm sure the look was achieved with a crimping iron and some back-combing, but I felt so betrayed that I liked to imagine the model had run afoul of a rabid squirrel.

In the hair and makeup trailer on my second film, rumors started to swirl about miracle flatirons from Japan. Previous generations of flatirons made your hair less curly yet somehow bigger and angrier, but not these. They were smaller, they were hotter, they'd transform you into the Amanda Bynes silk-nymph you'd always wanted to be (think *What a Girl Wants*, not mug shot). The cost of becoming this new woman? Almost two hundred dollars. (Straight-haired women, don't you judge me! Cheap curling irons are completely fine, but flatirons don't work like that!) The hair department bought one, and I used it on the days I had the energy for the Sisyphean task of straightening my hair, one inch at a time, knowing the process would begin anew upon the next wash. I had to get one for myself. I had no money, but you bet your ass I put that bad boy on a credit card. I couldn't go back to being Book Hermione when I'd had a taste of being Movie Hermione. If that reference went over your head: In the books, Hermione is supposed to be ugly. In the movies, she's Emma Watson. Also, in the book *she fixes herself with magic*. So nothing is fair.

You don't normally have your nails done on a film set. It's fine by me; I'm heavy-handed and I don't like sitting still, but I was recently talked into having biweekly manicures for a film. People will tell you that "gel manicures" won't ruin your nails as long as you change them out every two weeks, but if you ask me they are filthy liars. Maybe by the time this book comes out the gel manicure will be a thing of the past, like electrolysis or those Anna Nicole Smith diet pills I definitely never took. Just in case, please let me share my painful experience. I wore gel nails for three months on this movie, and when they finally came off, my boyfriend wouldn't let me touch him. My nails were so thin that they sliced and diced anything I came near. I was a human paper-cut factory.

I gain weight on every movie. Never ever have I left a set without putting on at least five pounds. You're not sleeping enough, you give up on exercise, and there is food EVERYWHERE. But the curse of the lady actor is to reach deep down, past the gurgling stomach acid, and find some willpower. When I'm trying to keep my ass in check, you'd think that fellow ladies would help me stay motivated. Instead, we end up torturing each other and ourselves. A group of hungry actresses (a.k.a. actresses) will talk about food with the kind of fervor and specificity normally found in *Star Trek* fan fiction. Some deep, hard-core stoner shit. Discussing food with girls on diets can feel eerily like porn dialogue.

"God, I would kill for a burger. Like a big, bloody cheeseburger on a brioche bun and some caramelized onions."

"Oooh, brioche? You're so bad. What about some bacon?"

"Fuck yeah, bacon."

"And some avocado . . . and grilled pineapple rings."

"Grilled pineapple? You pervert."

One Foot Out the Door

When you're a struggling actor, every job you get is a thrill and a relief. But unlike most professions, every job you get is temporary. The excitement is mired in the terror of knowing you'll be unemployed again in a matter of months. So even mid-movie you have to send out your résumé. For actors, that comes in the form of the self-tape. You can't make it to a casting office when you're shooting in the suburbs of Baltimore, so you and your castmates roll up your sleeves and put together a video in a trailer or a hotel room.

Rocket Science, my second film, was basically a sausage fest. Luckily, the young men in the cast were gentlemen of the highest order and fine actors to boot. On a day off, we all went to one cast member's hotel room to help him make a tape for a mafia movie. (We were young enough that this was an exciting project for all of us, not an obligation.) Aaron read lines offscreen, Nick operated the camera, Matt knew how to upload and send video. I didn't have a job to do, but I was happy to be there for moral support. True to any self-respecting mafia movie, there was a tremendous amount of shouting in the scene. We were all very impressed with the performance but wondered if the surrounding rooms were annoyed with the volume. Several takes in, there was a knock at the door. A take was still in progress, so I jumped up to go silence the curious party. *I'm helping!*

I gingerly whipped around the door without letting it completely shut behind me, like I'd seen crew members do when we were shooting. Outside was a stern-looking woman from hotel management who softened when she saw me. I held a finger to my lips, apologetic and pleading.

A man's angry voice was still emanating from inside, and now a teenage girl was desperately trying to get rid of the woman at the door. To someone who had no idea why hotel guests would be screaming for, you know . . . make-believe reasons, this development looked suspicious, to say the least. The hotel manager looked at me like, *Sister, if you're in trouble, I've got your back.* It was so courageous and supportive I was tempted to let her take care of me. I quickly remembered that this was real life and I figured ruining one take was worth it in this case. I threw the door open so she could see the collection of gangly young men filming their friend. Even in the throes of his heated performance, our resident artiste retreated from irate to meek instantaneously upon seeing the stranger at the door. We smiled nervously at the hotel manager. She looked us up and down.

"It sounds like you're killing each other in here. If you're gonna make your little movie in the rooms you have to be less *dramatic*."

Special Skills

Even low-budget films can be riddled with communication problems, and they only get worse and more frequent the larger the scale. As a result I have learned a number of specialized skills for absolutely no reason.

One film sent me to lessons on a horse farm for weeks. I wasn't learning to ride a horse, though, I was learning to sit *behind* someone riding a horse and not fall off. There wasn't actually a lot of skill involved. All you had to do was learn to spend an extended period of time clutching at someone's torso for dear life while galloping full speed, sans saddle or stirrups, on the aft of a sentient being (who weighed a literal half-ton and most days had a comically large erection).

I panicked during my first lesson because something was digging into my thigh and none of the instructors seemed that bothered about it. Saddles aren't made to have a passenger behind them, so when I mentioned my discomfort, there was a general attitude of "Yeah, that'll happen." When I pointed out the culprit, a metal ring about the circumference of a golf ball attached to the back of the saddle, my teacher frowned at it, gave it a tug, and said she'd try to take it off for my next lesson. Before you ask (believe it or not), I'm not the kind of gal who knows what purpose a metal ring might serve on the back of an English saddle, so no, I don't know what it was.

"It's just really digging into my leg, man. I'm not sure I can keep going."

"Well, I'm supposed to take you on at least five more runs. Do you want to take a five-minute break first? Maybe drink some water?" By the time I got home, I had a bruise on my thigh the size and color of a rotting mango.

At one point a renowned rider was brought in to work with me. A muscle-bound Spaniard who spoke almost no English, his connection with these horses seemed to transcend the laws of nature. On our first ride together we galloped past the stables through the rolling, sunlit hills. We took in the majesty of the countryside, and he turned back to me.

"Beautiful," he said.

"Yes, beautiful," I echoed.

He cast his dark eyes away from me and gave the horse a kick. I gripped his chest and buried my face in his neck as we picked up speed, all the while thinking, *When is this asshole gonna let me go home so I can ICE MY VAGINA?!*

The day of my big horse scene, as I perfected my mount and

dismount, the director said, "You know what, I'm never going to use that. I'm going to end the scene before you get on the horse."

So I hadn't learned to ride a horse, and as it turned out, there was no reason to spend all that time training my inner thighs to endure blunt force. But it wasn't a total waste. I got to be outside in pretty weather, and I've got a head start if I ever get into S&M.

I once played a chef, and although I did not get cooking lessons per se, I was sent to a knife skills course so that I'd *look* like I'd taken cooking lessons. In fact, I was flown from LA to Atlanta, more than once, on days that I didn't shoot anything, solely for more lessons. I chopped piles of herbs, diced mountains of onions, cored bushels of apples. I got confident but not especially good. This became clear when I sliced off a fingernail halfway through a pile of cilantro. Given the choice, I'd take a metal ring to the thigh any day.

When we set up the shot for my vegetable massacre, the director took a look at the monitor and called out, "Hey, Anna, don't worry about the chopping. We can't see your hands."

I've never driven a stick shift. Sidenote: I don't know why people act so superior about this. I don't churn my own butter, either; let's not act like I'm a dick for doing the easier thing. I was, however, asked if I would learn for the movie *The Voices*. The film was being shot in Germany, and the car that the producer chose, like most European cars, was manual. I expressed some hesitation but said that of course, if that's what needed to happen, I'd learn. For three days, before and after work, I drove a beat-up stick shift around a former Nazi airbase with a patient stuntwoman. Why a stuntwoman? I have no idea. The scene demanded that I start the car, then drive precisely ten feet, just out of frame. Not exactly "The Driver" from *The Driver*.

I joked to the producer that I was mostly worried about the other actress in the car. My scene partner, Gemma Arterton, happens to be a great beauty and a class-A broad, and the world would be cheated if we lost her to my poor driving skills.

"You're learning to drive a stick for that one shot?" The producer furrowed his brow. "That's ridiculous."

I was confused. Didn't he know that? Surely the days of lessons and the dozens of emails coordinating them couldn't have happened without the producer's knowledge. An hour later, I got an email saying that a nearly identical car, with automatic transmission, would be used for my driving scene. I am now pretty annoying about cutting out the middle man, a.k.a. ignoring the chain of command and bothering the person in charge of an entire film set about every little problem I have.

Cake Attack

On a recent film, we shot a scene in which a large wedding cake gets ruined. The characters all blame each other for the accident and pieces of the destroyed mass are lobbed back and forth in frustration. The fun part was that we had to shoot some of the aftermath before we shot the cake destruction itself. In order to create the conditions of a cake-fight aftermath, a cake-fight zone was constructed.

The art department commandeered a small room by the

kitchen of the rustic hotel we were shooting in. It was the last scene of the day, and after changing into my wardrobe I walked in, ready to be caked. Every surface was covered in clear plastic sheets. It was like something a serial killer would save on Pinterest under "Dream Office." If you walk into a room like this and you are not shooting a movie: Run, buddy! You are about to be dismembered!

I stood in the middle of the room and the director—a grown man, my creative ally—threw handfuls of heavily buttercreamed cake at me while I shrieked, further tickled by every frosted assault. At one point I started screaming, "Not the face! Not my beautiful face!!" Don't get too into a bit when you're wearing four-inch heels and standing in a pile of icing. I lost my balance and crashed to the Saran Wrapped–ground. At this point I was laughing so hard I couldn't breathe, so I barely noticed. Two members of the art department wearing lab coats (seriously, I was in Dexter's murderous paradise) helped me up and steadied me. Then they turned me around and held my arms so my *boss* could throw cake at my back. I squeezed my eyes shut and tried not to laugh and couldn't help but think, *I am in the world's weirdest, most precious porno right now.*

It Makes You Feel Like What?

I will also sometimes have to fake the use and subsequent effects of illegal substances. Sometimes that is not difficult because I've . . . got a good friend I can ask about it. Other times, it's a drug for which I have no point of reference outside of other actors depicting it on film.

I had to do several lines of fake cocaine in a heavily improvised film, so I asked around about how it would alter me. I've been around coke, I've been at many a party where I was the only person *not* doing coke, but I've never tried it myself. I once secretly rubbed some residue on my teeth because that's what people do in movies, but I didn't feel anything. I didn't have much to go on. Luckily, most people in LA had experience with it (and lots of places, actually; I remember conferring with other Maine expatriates after the first month of living elsewhere and confirming in disbelief that this was the norm. "Do people do *coke* where you are? I know!! Who does coke?! Have they not seen ANY movie?!").

It wasn't hard to find someone on set to walk me through it. So here's what I've got: cocaine makes you feel like the most important, most interesting person in the room. Why the hell would anyone do this drug? No, listen, it's your time on earth and I'm not here to judge anyone in this life (except people who don't like dogs—how do you not like dogs?), but that drug sounds horrible. Self-doubt is healthy! Self-doubt keeps me in check! It's the rare social interactions when I DON'T hate myself that keep me up at night.

Oh god. I just remembered the time in middle school when I thought I could pull off a wallet chain. I'm just—I'm just gonna crawl under the bed for a while.

Exploding Pig

Jake Szymanski, the director of *Mike and Dave Need Wedding Dates*, liked to call out direction during takes so we could work quickly and keep things spontaneous. One night, around four thirty in the morning, everyone in the cast was collectively covered in fake pig guts. The scene didn't make it into the film, and explaining the setup would take forever, so you'll just have to go with me here. It had been a long day, it was getting cold, and I don't know why, but the fake pig guts smelled awful. It was like someone tried to cover the smell of rotting garbage with a full jar of nutmeg, but it didn't quite work. Luckily, we were supposed to appear disgusted by them, but they really were rancid.

Jake was yelling out increasingly horrifying suggestions from the safety of his director's chair. They were all hilarious. But when he yelled, "Zac and Anna, get some of the chunks of pig guts in your mouth so you can spit them out!" Alice took over.

Hang on. A note about Alice, my character in *Mike and Dave*: I don't usually "take my characters home with me," which is a method-acting thing, not a sex thing. If it were a sex thing, I would do it. But Alice was a force to be reckoned with. She was hard to control. Maybe it was because we were doing so much improv or because Alice said the things I wasn't brave enough to say or because she's such an idiot. I like playing idiots. I tend to play smart, because I look smart. Let's be clear: it's not because I AM smart, I just "read" smart on camera. The two things are unrelated in actors.

I let Alice have free rein a lot during that shoot. When the "real" Mike and Dave Stangle came to visit the set, I spotted them across the lobby we were shooting in and yelled, "Get your dicks out!"

When they introduced themselves two days later, I pretended to be embarrassed about it, but I wasn't. Alice made me reckless and unflappable. So I was not going to be as docile as Zac.

So we're about to eat the fake pig guts— Hang on. A note about how sweet Zac Efron is: while we were making the movie, I was reading *The Rise and Fall of the Third Reich*. Zac struck up a conversation with me about my book and shared some stories about his Polish family coming to America during World War II. Then he took a breath to tell an anecdote he'd just remembered, but he stopped himself, like he'd thought better of it.

"I was going to tell you about this thing, but it happened toward the end of the war, so"—he smiled like a schoolboy with a secret—"I won't tell you yet." I followed his gaze down to my bookmark, nestled around the hundred-page mark.

"Zac, you know I know how it *ends*, right?"

"Yeah, but it'll be better if I wait." What a sweetheart.

So we're about to eat the fake pig guts— Hang on. A note about *The Rise and Fall of the Third Reich*: it's a tome of a book, an absolute monolith. Now, the *title* has an air of legitimacy, intellectual curiosity, even gravitas. However! Displayed on the cover of this beast, far more prominently than the title, is a huge, angry swastika. After a week of toting it around, I realized having a Nazi symbol clutched to my person everywhere I went looked . . . less than great. I got some electrical tape to cover it up and tried that for a day. Within an hour the tape started to peel off, and a small but unmistakable corner of the emblem emerged, like a shameful secret, which was SO MUCH WORSE. Kids, it's not the scandal; it's the cover-up.

SO we're eating fake pig guts, and by that I mean *Zac* is putting the fake pig guts in his mouth. What a trooper. I, on the other hand, get in full Alice mode and scream bloody murder across the pool at Jake.

"Why don't YOU get over here and put this putrid fucking mystery meat in YOUR mouth, you PIECE OF SHIT!"

I said that to my boss. And the crazy thing was, I don't think I was joking. Luckily for me, Jake laughed really hard anyway. Zac went for it, because he's a better person than me, and did a couple of really funny, really gross takes. He was so close to me, I could smell it from inside his mouth.

My god. How is he not throwing up right now?

And then he threw up. I was barefoot.

Sidebar: working with Zac Efron gave me a real-life understanding of how Charlie Manson got all those people to move to a ranch and do his bidding. Hear me out!

Last year I read this biography of Charlie Manson that managed to viscerally capture the atmosphere of the time and the mania of his followers. BUT I've still never been able to reconcile the whole "Yeah, but why did anyone follow this guy in the first place?" question. One week of knowing Zac and I got it.

Yes, Zac is unconscionably handsome, but I'm telling you that's not why people love him. (And I'm the first to discredit the achievements of the attractive and attribute their successes only to their physical appearance. Charming, aren't I?) People are just drawn to this guy. They behave like monkeys around him. Women behave like monkeys around most famous men, but it has more of a *Magic Mike*, aren't-I-being-naughty vibe. Women fawn over George Clooney and think they're being cute. Men fawn over famous guys in a bro-love way and usually want to show off by buying the guy a drink. But you know those movies where some remote culture sees a dude in armor for the first time and mistakes him for a god? It's like that with Zac.

People are drawn to Zac because he has the confidence of The Alpha. In Hawaii, I once watched a pack of local teenagers shadow him around a series of waterfalls like they were baby birds on the Discovery Channel. It was as if they had no choice in the matter. We'd gone to do some cliff diving, and every jump that Zac was willing to try was soon mounted by the rest of the onlookers. Even the muscle-bound tourists and the aloof locals couldn't help but steal a glance after they'd hit the water to see if Dad had been watching.

Based on his thrill-seeking recreational activities, I suspect some small part of Zac genuinely believes he's immortal. And honestly . . . he might be. That's probably what the magnetism is at its core. If there'd been an electrical surge, cutting off contact with the outside world, trapping us on the island forever, Zac Efron would have been the king of Oahu within forty-eight hours.

twilight

For those of you thinking, *Wait, she was in* Twilight*?*, I sure was! I was the sassy, awkward friend who broke up the relentless succession of intense stare-downs with musings on boys, tanning, and various school gossip. It was a sweet gig. The rest of the actors had to bring heart and honesty to fantasy situations involving life, death, eternal love, and the preservation of one's immortal soul. All I had to do was make jokes about how everyone was acting weird all the time.

The best part was that I got all the fun with none of the consequences! I got to show up to this mega-franchise for one to three weeks per movie, bear witness to the madness, and act like an idiot. I was once allowed to go on a rant about the zombie apocalypse genre (which was mostly a shout-out to Edgar Wright) and it actually ended up in the film. And I wasn't saddled with the creepy super-fame. Most of the cast couldn't walk out the door without being mobbed, but, weirdly, the vapid friend from school didn't inspire the same zeal in fans. None of the other filmmakers I worked with during those years had ever seen *Twilight*, but the series kept me in room and board while

I did their movies for no money. It was like the world's most ridiculous day job.

I have a vivid memory of my first day on the first movie. The cast and crew had been shooting for several weeks already and I was brought to the set to say hello to the director before my first scene the next day. Usually, a cast is happy to see additional characters; it's nice to get some new blood. Walking into the lunch tent felt like a scene from *Band of Brothers*. These were Toccoa men and I was the idiot greenhorn showing up like, "Hey, bros! Who's amped to get in there and rip it up?!"

Kellan Lutz is the sweetest guy, but that day I think he might have strangled me if he'd had the energy. Kristen Stewart—one of the most committed actors I've ever worked with—made a valiant effort to be friendly, but I could tell she was putting her back into it. Underneath every word, I heard *You don't know, man, you don't know what it's like out there.*

Wet and cold is not an environment conducive to making friends. Imagine if the first four weeks of a new job were spent outdoors in the freezing rain. Even when you all got to go inside, you'd just want to sleep and defrost your toes. You can't create many inside jokes when you're mostly numb. We were shooting in Oregon and Canada, in some of the most breathtaking locations I've ever seen. I would have enjoyed them more if I'd been in galoshes and a winter jacket. As it happened, we were pretending it was late spring, and after my first thirty minutes on set, ice-cold water had seeped through my Converse and saturated my cotton socks. Only fourteen hours to go!

On a small set, I might have had the luxury of a fluffy coat to run to before and after a scene. On *Twilight*, I was referred to most often as "Number 44." A coat wasn't in the cards.

I'd also like to mention the real MVPs of the *Twilight* movies: the background actors. Sometimes referred to as "extras," background actors have the most thankless job on set. By the fourth movie, old "Number 44" had at least earned ~~herself~~ itself a coat. But movie four was brutally cold. Especially the wedding scenes. Between shots the background actors stood around those space heaters that do almost nothing, but they didn't have winter coats. And they would come back the next day!

If you told me I had to be in that weather with no relief, I would have bailed like the little bitch I am. Extreme cold messes with you. The elements don't discriminate. And no amount of "you're getting paid to do this" matters when your body's basic survival requirements are in play. Someone once told me that the reason most Navy SEALs drop out isn't because of the physical demands or the danger, but because they don't want to be cold all the time anymore.

So now, when I'm standing in a patch of wet moss in open-toed shoes and a strapless chiffon sundress, watching my breath fog in front of my face (sometimes they try to make you suck on ice so they won't have to remove the fog in post—don't fall for it), I think: *You are a fucking Navy SEAL, Kendrick! You will get through this scene, you will say this stupid joke, and if you lose a nipple to frostbite in the process, it will be for art!!*

We shot that chilly wedding sequence in the forest outside of Squamish, British Columbia. Squamish had a population of about seventeen thousand people and, as far as I could tell, only one hotel capable of housing a film crew. The production company rented out the whole place.

The hotel was set back from the road and surrounded by grassy fields. My room was on the lobby level and faced the back of the grounds, overlooking a little lake and thick woods that started about a football field's length from my window. It was probably quite pretty in the summer, or the deep winter, but muddy early spring gave it a foreboding quality. The only book I brought with me, I swear on my life, was *The Shining*.

It was a large hotel, much larger in fact than our crew needed, so the place was eerily empty. Renting out every room seemed like overkill, but by the time we made *Breaking Dawn*, the Twilight-mania had reached critical mass. Certain precautionary measures had to be taken for the security of the cast and crew. So it was just us. The lonely patients of an expansive asylum.

At least twice a day, someone I didn't recognize would be in the lobby, getting kicked out as they protested that they *really were* waiting for a friend. The hotel staff knew no one was staying there but the cast and crew, and none of us had invited friends up, because no one wants to come to Squamish.*

I struck up a conversation with the receptionist and she said they were trying to stop people before they got onto the grounds, but the more innocuous-looking ones slipped through. The paparazzi, on the other hand, knew that legally they had to

---

* Beautiful country up there, I highly recommend a visit. Perhaps with a non–Stephen King novel.

stay past the end of the long drive. She pointed down the road to five black SUVs, parked and running, just at the entrance to the hotel. *Ho. Ly. Shit.* I hadn't even noticed them before!

I stayed in my room. The paps didn't care about me—they were there for the Kristens and Robs of the world—but it was creepy knowing they were out there. Inside, I had nothing to do. The internet didn't work and the TV was . . . Canadian TV, so against my better judgment, I read *The Shining*.

Our wrap party was that weekend. I felt like I hadn't really earned the right to go to the wrap party, considering I showed up to film my entire role in the last two weeks, but I was happy to get out of the room. The wrap party was at the restaurant in the hotel, thirty feet from my room. Fair enough, and still counts! I had a few drinks, heard some stories about paparazzi caught sneaking around the back field, and after a while someone offered me some weed.

The paranoia came quickly, so I excused myself. Thank god my room was on the same floor; I wouldn't have made it through an elevator ride without having a full-on claustrophobic breakdown. I got into my room and double-locked the doors. Then it hit me that being on the ground floor, overlooking those ominous woods, was not ideal in my current state, either. I couldn't decide if having the curtains closed or open was more terrifying. Paranoia is one thing, but when people are actually watching you, it's hard to talk yourself off a ledge. I paced manically across the room, alternately looking through the peephole and the curtains on the back window. Why had I smoked weed in this creepy hotel? Why had I smoked weed after reading *The Shining* all day? Why did I read *The Shining* in this creepy hotel?!

I woke up the next morning to find all my luggage and a few pieces of furniture piled against the door.

Chat, Die, Repeat

The best part of *Breaking Dawn* (and maybe the whole series) was when we shot a dream sequence in which I was a dead body. It was so much fun! And inside a room-temperature studio! Kristen's character has a nightmare in which she imagines she is marrying her beloved—totally normal, nothing weird going on—only to discover that she is standing on a veritable funeral pyre of her closest friends and family! (Man. Those movies got dark.)

Before shooting, everyone in the scene had to line up in their perfectly white dream-sequence outfits and get sprayed down with fake blood. That was someone's job for the day, to be fake-blood-spray-down guy. Each of us then climbed into a preordained nook in an enormous pile of bloody mannequins. My nook was toward the top of the pile, near the happy couple, giving the impression that I was just underfoot. It was actually pretty comfortable, and I chatted with Kristen and Rob from my prostrate position. Then we'd hear "rolling" and "action" and I'd hold my breath and fix my eyes on one spot. Then I'd go back to chatting with Kristen, occasionally making sure that the actors pressed around and under me weren't too uncomfortable.

The spray-down had apparently not been thorough enough, and after a few takes, a stocky crew member in hiking boots climbed up the pile and poured blood on us from a bucket. It was so awesome.

Covered in blood, but her foundation is flawless.
Movies make sense.

big breaks

Up in the Air, a.k.a. Everything Is Amazing, Everything Is on Fire

I spent the first few weeks shooting *Up in the Air* certain that I'd be fired at any moment. I'd start to silently spiral before an important scene and George Clooney would have to snap me out of it, usually by throwing something near my head. George has been famous for a long time and knows the effect he has on people. He has a skill for making situations feel relaxed and informal, and keeping you in the moment.

About halfway through the shoot we all went to dinner, and for the ninety seconds of the evening where George wasn't dutifully chatting with excited restaurant patrons, I made small talk with him about the scenes we had shot so far. He laughed a little and expressed some reluctance to talk about how it was going because he didn't want to get in my head.

"I shouldn't say anything. I mean, no one wants me to say anything because, you know, you don't talk to your guy when he's pitching a no-hitter."

Not being a baseball fan I only vaguely understood this comment to mean I was doing well, but since it was exactly the kind of thing that might have gotten in my head, I decided not to look it up.

I left the shoot happy and proud and I couldn't wait to show the film to my parents and my friends and the rest of the world. I had zero suspicions that it would be an "awards film." It seemed so light to me, so intimate. Oscar films are epic! They deal with war, and death, and destruction! Of course, plenty of Oscar-winning films are about regular people in everyday settings; I just truly hadn't thought about it that much. I was wholly unprepared for what came next.

When the movie premiered at the Toronto Film Festival, someone told me things were about to get "loud and fast" for a while. Turns out loud and fast wasn't how it would feel. It felt like being one of those frogs that doesn't notice the water is boiling until she's standing in the middle of a hotel room crying in socks and a stick-on bra. From September 2009 through February 2010, I was on a nonstop promotional tour in support of the film. During those six months, *Up in the Air* debuted to critical acclaim, I was nominated for an Academy Award, and I finally saw that video of the baby panda sneezing. Not a bad half year. Yet it was perhaps the most confusing period of my life.

The press for *Up in the Air* was a beast because it was all so serious. I didn't want to let anyone down, so I tried to take it just as seriously as everyone else. You can't imagine how soul-crushing it was for my misanthropic ass to be sincere for six months.

I didn't know what I was doing. But the stakes seemed unbearably high. When everyone around you is acting like *this* is the most important thing in the world, you start to believe them. Nowadays, if you need me to do a "radio tour," which is essentially three hours on the phone giving sound bites to various shows around the country, I'll probably clean my bathroom mid-interview and mention my vagina at least once. If you throw me in a room full of "tastemakers" (whatever that means, I still don't know), I'll turn on my personal brand of awkward, sarcastic schmooze and hope for the best, because *now* I understand that they might love me, they might hate me, but no one's gonna die.

But back then, each successive task felt like the most critical thing I would ever do. Every event was an anxiety-inducing clusterfuck or an exercise in solitude and tediousness. Now, I know it's all a farce. I know how to snap myself out of it. *This is not hard! This is not forced manual labor or the Cuban Missile Crisis!* At the time, the pressure of these unfamiliar situations rattled my already shoddy emotional equilibrium.

There actually was a weird side effect. I was in sound-bite pageant mode so much that I started compulsively saying deeply honest, often inappropriate things to people I'd just met. I had to come up for air. The only people I was interacting with at the time were fancy folks at fancy events, but if you weren't a journalist, you were probably going to hear about my most recent sex dream. I'm sure these people just wanted a nice evening out and perhaps some sparkling banter from the young actress. What they usually got was an earful on my fear of mortality. People ask me now if I get nervous about being "too" honest on social media. The alternative is much more terrifying. The crazy wants out.

I felt like a fraud! I was being flown around, staying in hotels I could never afford and putting on clothes that someone else picked out. When I went home, I dragged a suitcase full of those items I didn't own across my tar-stained carpet and dumped it out at the foot of my Ikea bed.

Each time I locked the door to my squalid apartment, I grew more fearful that my filthy secret would spill out: I am—at *best*—a normal human, and this has all been a big misunderstanding. A lot of people were devoting a lot of energy to maintaining the illusion that I was the ready-made ingenue. It made me feel disingenuous and guilty. I was participating in a con.

Sometimes I found it all too funny for words. I'd be at an afternoon tea in the penthouse suite of the Chateau Marmont wearing some boatneck sundress and think, *Two years ago I choreographed a fake music video to "Fergalicious" with two drunk strippers in this very room. This is a joke!* Other times it was harder to find the humor.

The trickiest parts were the constant assurances that I was having a great time. I'm not an idiot. I knew what was happening was positive, it just got . . . disorienting. I don't mind hard work—I love a challenge!—but pretending everything is wonderful when it's not makes me feel mentally ill.

I was expending all this energy, but I wasn't creating anything, I wasn't learning anything, and my job became convincing the world that I was off having the adventure of a lifetime. I did it well enough that my own mother bought it. When I stopped answering her calls she got upset with me. She assumed I thought I was too cool to talk to her now. In reality, I couldn't pick up the phone because I knew the second I heard her voice I'd finally let go and burst into tears.

Once I talked to my mom (and did indeed break down crying), she completely understood why I hadn't been in touch. That didn't stop her from guilting me into taking her to the Oscars. When the show was over she looked shell-shocked. "I can't believe you've been doing that for six months. I'm never doing that again."

The highs and lows were so extreme! Just when I'd reach a tipping point—convinced that I'd become nothing more than a commodity, disgusted with myself for taking this artistic experience, which had been so fulfilling, and packaging it up to be sold in pieces to people who couldn't care less about me—something amazing would happen. I was trudging up the steps to my apartment when I got an email with the subject line: Dreams Do Come True. I walked through my door and onto my tar-stained carpet and opened it. It was Peter Travers's review for *Rolling Stone*. It read: *Kendrick is a revelation*. I stood on that tar stain and wept.

I was a revelation, but I was still broke. At the end of one New York press tour I asked Paramount if I could stay in a less expensive hotel on the next trip and . . . keep the difference. They said no because "that's not how it works." I wanted to know why that wasn't how it worked, but I could tell I'd already embarrassed myself, so I dropped it. Then I stole a roll of toilet paper out of the bathroom and put it in my suitcase because I knew I wouldn't have the time or energy to buy any when I got home.

When reporters asked how I was handling my "new fame," I tried to make a joke of it. "Well, I still go to sleep in the same bed as before this happened." It always sounded like a platitude. Like "I still put my pants on one leg at a time" or "My friends and family keep me grounded" (yawn). But I literally meant, *Nothing has changed. In fact, Mr. Journalist, the insecurity I feel about the Grand Canyon–size gap between my real life and people's expectations is giving me relentless anxiety, so if we could just cool it, that would be great. I stole a roll of toilet paper this week. You can see how "fame" wouldn't be going to my head.*

If I'd been allowed, even once, to say, "Hey, I'm having kind of a shitty day," I think I would have been *fine*. If my dad had been there to give me that look like, "These people are crazy," I would have been able to handle anything. But admitting that I was lost and overwhelmed felt *so* ungrateful. Imagine if during final exams, everyone in your life was saying, "Finals are here! This is the best your life is ever going to get!" On top of being exhausted and grumpy, you'd feel guilty about your own, very human emotions. (And probably in crisis because *Dear god, what if this IS the best life ever gets?!*) This is why we talk about our feelings!

About a week before Oscar nominations were announced I went to New York to do a talk show. Afterward my brother and I walked around the city in the dark for a while. I knew he wouldn't judge me, so after a while I said, "Everyone keeps telling me that I'm gonna . . . which I feel like they shouldn't, you know . . . because . . . I mean, am I going to wake up next week disappointed that I'm not an Oscar nominee? 'Cause I've been *not an Oscar nominee* my whole life and I've been okay." Saying it felt better. Then just for good measure I added, "And you know what, some of these other people look VERY at home being feted and adored and it's creepy and I think they're fuckin' charlatans." Being a little bit petulant felt better, too.

The very last piece of press I did for *Up in the Air* was in Tokyo. The movie was released in Japan several months after the US release and a little while after the Oscars. I got to run around Tokyo for a day, which was INCREDIBLE. The following two days were jam-packed with interviews. During one roundtable, the lone English-speaking journalist said, "I've been following the press that you're doing and it seems like different publications are writing their own version of you. You know, you're like the overwhelmed newcomer or the independent, serious artist or the mainstream, commercial star. Do you feel pressured to play along with what they want? Do you ever feel like you're lying?"

Maybe it was because it was the end of my tour or because he was a fellow American in Japan so I was having a bullshit *Lost in Translation* moment, or maybe because if I'd suppressed the crazy for one more second I would have ruptured something.

"Honestly? Some part of everything I've said in the last six months has been a lie."

He laughed. "Including that?"

"Yes," I said, totally serious.

Fame Changes Everything, a.k.a. I'm in *Vogue* but I Still Don't Have a TV

Fame did change things. For example, when you Googled "Anna Kendrick," the second wife of colonial New Hampshire governor Benjamin Pierce (also named Anna Kendrick) was no longer the first result. Make it raaaaaaaaain!

The other new development was that strangers got real friendly and said hello to me and asked for pictures. And that's the end of the list. ☺

Fame doesn't change much else. It doesn't change how you feel about your high school "nemesis" or how your passive-aggressive uncle treats you (it just shifted from "Maybe if you got a real job you could afford a car that doesn't break down every week" to "Well, we can't all be Hollywood actresses who eat gold and poop caviar"). And believe me, I was *loath* to discover fame wasn't changing me. I really hoped that I'd be transformed into a benevolent, self-possessed woman. Even when I got nominated for an Oscar, I was still just an anxious, jaded procrastinator. Maybe we all have imposter syndrome and perpetually feel like our real life is right around the corner, and if daily (often unearned) praise from strangers didn't help me out with that, I guess we've all just got to put in the work.

The incident that really should have made me insufferably smug only confirmed to me that I was a squirrelly little weirdo. A few months after the Oscars, I ran into the prettiest girl from my high school on a trip home. She approached me in the street, and we chatted for barely thirty seconds before the conversation petered out. Then I noticed her bag.

"Oh hey, I have that purse."

"I know," she said, "I got it because of you."

This should have felt so satisfying! Instead my stomach lurched at the batshit-crazy notion that people I used to know could find out what kind of purse I was carrying at any given moment. And that they would then buy it! I want to go back to being the loser in the corner, please!

But maybe I was reading too much into it. Besides, it's not like the fact that she bought this bag meant she'd had some moment of clarity where she'd realized the short, frizzy-haired girl from high school wasn't a total freak after all. She probably just saw a picture on the internet one day and went, "I think that girl is from my hometown. Cute bag." Or maybe she's obsessed with me and has a lock of my hair under her pillow. Who can say?

Don't Look a Paparazzo in the Eye and Other Lessons I Learned the Hard Way

Junkets

A press junket is a full day of interviews to promote one film. The film studio or distribution company will rent out a number of hotel rooms, stick you in one, and bring in upward of seventy journalists to talk to you, one at a time. Every first-time junketer will come out of their room around lunchtime and say something like "They're all asking the same questions, can't we just give the answers *once* and they could all share it?" The mistake there is the assumption that anyone is interested in the answers. This is not *Meet the Press*; no one is dying to hear about how we related to our characters. You are an actor, and they need hits for their website; let's all do our part in an orderly fashion and go home.

At first I found junkets disturbing because I thought the reporters were patronizing me. I've been sensitive to people talking down to me my whole life because I look young. When someone spoke to me like I was twelve, I would think, *This motherfucker thinks I'm some idiotic little actress and they have to talk to me like a Miss USA contestant.* I'd get all huffy about it. At my first Golden Globes I overheard an interview happening next to me and realized, *Dear god, they're talking to Dame Helen Mirren in that same sugary, condescending tone.* So now it's annoying, but I don't take it personally.

Some on-camera journalists are so cheesy it's jarring. I had never noticed it when I heard their voices on TV: "Coming up! We're gonna chat with the owner of YouTube's newest furry sensation: Reginald the mongoose!" I get why they use the voice: it feels right on TV, it keeps the audience engaged, and they are doing the right thing to use it! But in person, it's shocking how unnatural their demeanor is. Every time I talk to one of these journalists—every *single* time—I picture them having sex. I don't mean to, it just happens! I can't stop myself! What is it like?! Do they have that same crazy energy? Are they like, "I mean, *wow*, Janet, this lovemaking is just sensational!" It's all I'm thinking about. (Unless I do an interview and someone asks me about this part of the book, in which case, I'm obviously just joking.) *(I'm not just joking.)*

And it can't be easy for the journalists. It's not their fault the studio scheduled them as interview sixty-one out of seventy. Just like it's not my fault that by interview sixty-one I'm playing a game with myself where I try to sneak the word "kerfuffle" into every answer as a mental exercise to stave off the creeping madness.

It's the day of a million questions, yet somehow it's the same questions over and over. It's like babysitting a toddler (but at least you can shake a toddler). Fatigue and repetition mess with you. That's why they make great "enhanced interrogation" techniques. In fact, when trying to extract confessions from criminal masterminds, I'd recommend putting them in hair extensions, heels, and individual false eyelashes. They'll tell you EVERY-THING.

Print

Print is a rude awakening. Seeing your conversational speech written down forces you to acknowledge how many lexical gaps you fill with phrases like "stuff," "thingy," "whatever," and "urggsssghhh, ya know?"

In every print interview I do, I resolve to speak as though I were writing. It lasts four minutes, tops. Without fail I feel like a pretentious douche who speaks slower than Alan Rickman, and I revert to fast-paced colloquialisms because I'd rather save face in front of this one reporter than the rest of the world. I end up reading what I said, thinking, *Am I THAT bad at communication?* I'm going to be a nightmare in my inevitable marriage counseling.

Print interviews are also a mindfuck because this person is going to write up not only what you say, but how you *seem* as you say it, and how you seem as you pause, and how you seem as you walk in. You become so self-conscious about every mannerism, so aware of trying *not* to act self-aware, it can feel like you are trying to disprove a negative. Jon Ronson's book *The Psy-*

chopath Test says that if you are accused of being a psychopath, it's incredibly difficult to prove that you aren't one. Psychopaths are masters of mimicking healthy human behavior, so how does a real, healthy human prove that they aren't faking it?

But here's the thing: I *am* faking it. It's an interview; the very construct is artificial. It's a manufactured conversation. If anything, *I* make the mistake of buying into it more than a decent journalist ever would. Sometimes I think the writer and I are becoming friends, because they are such a good listener. (I know, guys, I'm not very bright.)

So, aren't we both faking? And I get it, journalists; you aren't dying to talk to every ego-bloated actor who rolls through town, you do it because it's part of your job. You ACT thrilled about it because of the social contract, and so do I! But I'm not thrilled. We just met! I'd have to be insane to be "thrilled" to talk about myself with a perfect stranger knowing that they plan to make every word of it available to every other human on the planet.

There are some journalists I've known for a few years now and I always like talking to them. There are some who I meet and get along with because they are good at their job, and the fact that I feel comfortable immediately is solely a testament to them. Sometimes the ones who seem really unhappy to be there write very kind things, and the ones who seem really friendly write very passive-aggressive things. I once developed a crush on a journalist after spending less than twenty minutes with him. It wasn't a physical thing; he was just good at his job, so I felt like we were having a good time.

Afterward I admonished myself for thinking I had a "connection" with someone who is quite literally paid to be interested in me. He described me in his piece as though I was a robot capable of turning my "press face" on and off. The interview psychopath! This was one of the rare times I'd been completely caught up in the conversation—embarrassingly so—yet I'd been accused of being a big fat faker. What are you gonna do? I guess I should be grateful he didn't say, "Fellow journalists: beware. This dummy clearly wanted to bone me."

Photo Shoots

For one of my first big photo shoots, the *Vogue* team took me to the outskirts of Brooklyn. They were putting me in a feature they do every month that's like, *Hey, you don't know this girl yet but she's cool. Trust us. We're* Vogue. They gave off major "cool girl" vibes, and I needed to be friends with them immediately, so when they wanted to photograph me under a bridge that had clearly been roped off, I agreed. Once we were through the layers of plastic sheeting I realized it had been shut down because of a burst pipe. A pipe of what? I guess I'll find out if and when I develop conditions consistent with radiation poisoning.

Sometimes I like to run around photo shoots all carefree and wild, as a layer of protection. When I stay still and focus all my attention and energy on being the best little model I can be and *still* I get looks of disappointment and confusion because I don't look like Kendall Jenner, it hurts my tiny feelings. (You can go your whole life as a happy, sane person, and then Kendall Jenner comes up and you wonder why you want to crawl into a hole and rot. No one should be compared to Kendall Jenner. It's cruel and unusual.) So I run around a little. *I'm not an unphotograph-able troll! I'm just a little scamp who's not focused!*

When I behave, I find myself in the line of fire for innocuous comments that lodge in my brain and explode like tiny, hateful pipe bombs right before I fall asleep. The photographer for one artsy magazine told me to relax my shoulders, twenty-one times. (I'd always thought my shoulders were fine.) A photographer for a men's mag asked, "Can we lose the bra?" in a tone that felt as rhetorical as "Can you get that report on my desk by Friday?" When he saw me glance at the monitor, he said, "Don't worry, we'll slim out your legs." (I'd always thought my legs were fine.)

I have one piece of advice for photographers. I know you have no reason to listen to advice from me, but please, it's good for everyone. If you are photographing an actress, or a bride, or a recent graduate who doesn't have the jaded, knowing sensibility of a model, please just take lots of pictures and say lots of nice things. None of you shoot on film anymore! It costs you nothing to just keep snapping away and shouting praise! It's like teaching a little kid to hit a baseball. You don't stand there and stare at him like, *This little chump isn't even using a regulation bat.* You throw the ball and say "good job," and eventually he hits one. That technique won't help A-Rod improve his batting average, but I'm not A-Rod—I'm the little kid with the Styrofoam bat who can't see 'cause the helmet's too big.

Paparazzi

Generally speaking (knock on wood) I don't have many prob-lems with paparazzi. Occasionally I'll see a photo of myself online that I didn't know was being taken. It's unsettling. Usually, I'm just worried I got caught picking my nose. So far, so good, but keep me in your prayers!

When *Up in the Air* came out, there was a period where some paparazzi staked out my apartment. Of course, I didn't know this for a while. The first time I spotted a paparazzo was in the basement of an Ikea in Burbank. I'd gone to get some storage boxes (the all-time greatest stress-relieving activity), and about half an hour into my shopping trip I looked up from my cart and saw a man taking photos of me.

Okay, I thought, *so this is it, this is the first time this happens.*

I put my throw pillows into the cart (yes, I know I was there to get storage boxes; perhaps you don't understand how Ikea works) and walked over to him. He put his camera down. He looked bewildered but not defensive, like this wasn't normal, but he didn't anticipate a Colin Farrell situation.

I pulled on the sleeves of my hoodie. "Hi. Um . . . how did you . . ." *Know I'd be here? Find me?* It all sounded so espionage. He knew what I meant.

"Oh, I was just in here."

I knew that didn't sound right, but I was so out of my element, I just accepted that he happened to be in the basement of Ikea with his long-lens camera at the same time I was.

He nodded sympathetically. "Oh right, you're new to the game."

Ew.

I wasn't offended in a righteous indignation way, like, *My life is not some* game*!* It was just a cringey thing to say.

I suppressed an eye roll and said, "Right, so . . . what happens now? Are you gonna, like, follow me around the store?"

"If I can get a good shot of you now, I'll just leave, no problem. I promise I won't follow you home."

Follow me home. I hadn't even thought of that.

Letting this guy take my picture so that he would go away seemed like the path of least resistance, so I went back to my cart and stood there.

"Grab something off the shelf, and you can look up like you just spotted me. Don't smile or anything, you can look annoyed."

Yeah, I'll try to manage that.

He took the picture, and, true to his word, he left. He called someone else from his agency to follow me home, so technically, he kept his promise. For the next three weeks or so, someone was outside my apartment. What they didn't count on was my god-given ability to stay indoors and do nothing. The real beauty of it was I didn't even have to alter my behavior. I wasn't holed up Waco-style; I was just doing me. Every now and then a similar thing will happen. I'll notice a strange car outside, and, as an experiment, I'll take a trip to Home Depot, and when the car follows me, I think, *Looks like a two-week stretch of takeout and Netflix is in order; this poor man doesn't know who he's dealing with.*

On Being Nice

The word "nice" means a couple different things for me now. In one area of my life, I can earn this descriptor very easily, almost too easily. People I meet who want to say hello or take a picture often say, "You're so nice." Don't worry—never once have I deluded myself into thinking I've done something to deserve this compliment. It's often said after a twenty-second interaction at a restaurant or in a hotel lobby. I could have no other redeeming qualities, but I'm "nice" as long as I haven't crippled a bellboy.

Don't get me wrong, I find it incredibly sweet that anyone would say it, and I get that maybe they don't mean anything more than "Thanks" but it comes out "You're so nice." Plus, people have said some weird-ass shit to me over the years, so I will take "You're so nice" ANY day.

In a professional sense, "nice" is harder to earn. Harder for me anyway. Because "nice" often means she did what we told her to, no questions asked. I've seen nice defined as: *In working with XXXXX, I encountered no conflict which might have forced me to acknowledge this person as a fellow human capable of discomfort or creative input.* Not all people in my industry feel this way— certainly none of the people I've talked about in this book—but many do. This is highlighted by the fact that, in the professional realm, the opposite of nice is not "mean"; the opposite of nice is "difficult."

Ninety percent of the people I've worked with who are disruptive or lazy or unskilled or addicts or likely to throw a tantrum are men. Ninety percent of the ones who get called "difficult" are women. Lest we be besmirched with that most damning label, it feels imperative that we strive for "nice." When I'm put in an uncomfortable position or when someone asks something of me that I feel borders on taking advantage, the threat of "so nice" being snatched away from me hangs in the air. Should I stand my ground, or be a doormat? How many concessions would I have to make, how much crap would I have to swallow to stay a "nice girl"? Usually more than I am willing.

Women encounter this in social situations as well. *Let me take you out. Don't be so uptight. Just have one more drink.* And if you don't, someone might strip you of an adjective you've been convinced has value, and label you as something else. Professional people are usually clever enough not to use this term, but in social situations, the threatened brand is "bitch."

As Sondheim said, *Nice is different than good.* Do you need to do whatever you're told to be a nice person? Maybe. Do you need to do whatever you're told to be a good person? Of course not! Man, woman, personal, professional—some people have a skill for persuading you the best thing you can be is obedient.

A woman I was about to work with told me she'd been asking around about me. She said someone described me as "ten percent defiant." She was quick to point out she didn't think they'd meant it as a criticism. I was quick to point out I didn't take it as one.

I gave up on being Nice. I started putting more value on other qualities instead: passion, bravery, intelligence, practicality, humor, patience, fairness, sensitivity. Those last three might seem like they are covered by "nice," but make no mistake, they are not. A person who smiles a lot and remembers everyone's birthday can turn out to be undercover crazy, a compulsive thief, and boring to boot. I don't put a lot of stock in nice. I'd prefer to be around people who have any of the above qualities over "niceness," and I'd prefer it if that applied to me, too. I'm also okay if the most accurate description of me is *nervous, and a little salty.* But at least I know what I want to strive for.

award shows

An award show isn't glamorous. It's the closest I'll ever get to glamorous, so I'm not knocking it, but I know it's not the real deal. Real glamour is opening night at the opera, or a lavish wedding on a tropical cliffside. I assume; I've never been invited to either of those things. An award show is as glamorous as a middle school dance. Again, I assume; I was never invited to a middle school dance, either. Industry fetes are populated with nervous idiots in the nicest clothes they could find and beleaguered chaperones in black jeans and blazers trying to make sure the nervous idiots don't accidentally set the place on fire before the night is over.

I usually arrive to major events with a mild injury from maintaining the "wrinkle-free" position in the car on the way there. A stylist will have steamed my dress to smooth, buttery perfection, and there's nothing like a long car ride to give you a nice erratic patch of creases just above your crotch, so you brace yourself like a corpse in a diagonal position on your seat. You must not bend at the waist! If there's no one sitting next to you, you can lie across two seats, but even *my* body is not short enough to fit that way, so you're up on your elbows the whole time. You'll be in this position for about half an hour, so choose wisely. Oh, and my favorite thing about this technique is that it doesn't work.

Getting out of the car is always a little fun, I'll admit, because I like to go out the "wrong" side. This is a HUGE deal for no reason at all and I get a rush of mischievous pleasure every time I do it. The event organizers want you to get out on the side where the red carpet is set up so that photographers can get the "coming out of the car" shot. That shot is universally awful. Even if there's no possibility of an up-skirt, I've *just* contorted my body back to a recognizable human position and all the blood is returning to my fingers; let's not capture that for posterity. Without fail, the headset-clad representative who has been sent to begin chaperoning me will open the car door to find me exiting the other side and start sputtering that I need to get out on this side, on this side! But it's too late, and ten seconds later when I am beside them (because like Bear Grylls or the dog in *Homeward Bound*, somehow I persevered and made it to my destination), even they seem confused about why their heart rate is so elevated. And then the shouting begins.

The good shouting is from people who have come to take pictures on their phones and mid-range digital cameras. They are friendly and sincere and when I wave at them they cheer, and I won't lie, I feel like I'm a slightly taller Kim Jong-un and it's dope as hell. At the big award shows you stand between the fans and the line of photographers, and I like to swing around every couple of steps and make ugly faces at the friendly side to remind myself that we're all just pretending. I often regret it because someone in the crowd catches a photo that ends up on-line, but it's the price I pay to keep my public happy! (Sorry . . . it goes to your head fast. I would make a great ruthless dictator.)

The bad shouting is from the line of photographers. They don't want a good picture, they *need* a good picture. This is their job, and "Over here! Smile! Tell us who you're wearing!" is not a request floated by a fan; it's a demand. They are traders on the floor of the New York Stock Exchange and they will be heard, dammit.

"Buy! Sell! Over here! Over the shoulder! Over the shoulder, Anna! Show us the back of the dresssssssss!" You must maintain your smile through it, though. You cannot give any indication that a hundred people are shouting at you like drowning victims begging for a lifeboat. And when they say "Blow us a kiss!"— don't do it. First of all, the photograph won't have a caption that says, "Some red-faced photographer asked her to do this—she didn't just walk up to the red carpet and think, *How can I make myself look like an asshole?*" And second, your eyes always half close when you blow a kiss, which makes you look drunk. This is especially frustrating when you managed to limit your intake to four drinks pre-carpet. Get good at saying "No thank you" through clenched teeth. Otherwise, they'll get a photo where you look scowly, and *In Touch Weekly* will use it the next time they want to imply your husband is cheating on you with your dog psychic.

After photos, you talk to some on-camera journalists. I have probably given my worst sound bites on red carpets. Cameras are going off, people are screaming, Grumpy Cat shows up. There should be special training for this, like they did with horses in the First World War.

More than once I have literally bailed three words into a response. "Yeah, it's exciting to be here, uh . . . I don't, uh, I'm bad at this, I'm sorry." I have said those words verbatim. Why do they keep inviting me back?

There's a campaign called #AskHerMore, which was started by some thoughtful, intelligent females (Lena Dunham, Reese Witherspoon, Shonda Rhimes, etc.). It aims to ensure that when women attend events, they are asked about more than their dresses. Men don't answer questions exclusively about their clothes; why should we? A simple and understandable request.

However, if people could ask *me* less, that would be great. I would love it if we could limit my red carpet topics to my favorite colors, what sound a duck makes, and my thoughts on McDonald's All-Day Breakfast—blessing or curse?

The next step is finding someone you know. Once I find someone who is willing to talk to me, I don't leave their side for the rest of the evening. Unless I find someone better. Then I'm like, "God, some loser named Chris Pine has been following me around all night, let's shake him!"

Meeting someone new in these situations is odd, because you don't normally meet someone for the first time in a gown or a tuxedo. The clothes have a strange effect on my speech, and unless I know the person very well I take on a mannered, old-timey tone. I find myself asking men things like "May I take your arm?" instead of saying, "Dude, my heels are a shit show, so

I'm gonna hold on to you, 'cause if I don't I'm gonna drop faster than anything I've ever been handed that's over ten pounds."

Another source of anxiety is the famous people! The fucking famous people everywhere! Handsome movie stars, beautiful movie stars, young movie star couples I suspect are only together for the PR. (For the record, if I was approached to be the girlfriend of a male celebrity for a few months for PR purposes, I would one hundred percent do it. That's not a joke; I wouldn't even hesitate.)

Even when you are nominated for an award, or chatting with your movie star cast, the other celebrities at award shows reduce you to the most pathetic version of yourself. You know that feeling when you see a pretty girl and you immediately hate her because you assume she'd never talk to you (this metaphor works if you're a girl or a guy), but then she smiles and introduces herself and you're like, how could I have misjudged you, you are clearly the best person alive! That feeling is intensified tenfold with movie stars. *Ugh, look at Kate Beckinsale across the room with her perfect hair and her perfect laugh and I'll bet she's an ice queen bitc— Oh god, she's coming over here.* She gives you a compliment and tells you one dirty joke and you are ready to blindly pledge your life to her service. Long live the queen!

After a while you'll have to pee, and that's where the illusion really falls apart. Even the nicest gown can't be glamorous when you've got it hiked around your waist. Why even steam the dress?! You're holding up the full skirt with one hand (sometimes the dress is so big it fills the entire stall) while you use the other to get your underwear down. You are pigeon-toed in your six-inch heels and it's a miracle if you make it through the ordeal rip- and urine-free.

The show itself is usually funny, but no one laughs because we are all hungry and nervous. Sometimes you get to meet someone unexpected and delightful—for example, at my first Golden Globes I met the voice of Dug from the film *Up*, and he indulged me by saying, "I have just met you and I *looove* you." I know! The after-party is often better, because win or lose, it's over, and you can find something to eat! Actually, watching gorgeous women in skintight gowns attacking anyone holding a tray of food is half the fun.

The best part is going home. It's a relief. I'm so happy it's over, which I know sounds like a line. It's not like I'm NOT checking Twitter to see if people liked my dress, but there's an afterglow when my anxiety level returns to its normal, low-grade panic setting and simple acts are transformed into considerable luxuries.

I usually take off my shoes in the car and walk into my home barefoot, my dress dragging. The dress comes off and I get into sweatpants and a hoodie with no bra, but for the moment I keep on the jewelry and makeup. If the event is out of town and I'm staying in a hotel, I get into the bathrobe, which is nice, but it still has a Marilyn Monroe, glamorous vibe, and I'm going for more of a trashy jewel thief thing.

At home I get to sit on my couch, put on an old episode of *30 Rock*, and eat mac and cheese in sweatpants and thousands of dollars' worth of diamonds. It is the most delicious dichotomy I've encountered in my life.

Voyeur

My first big award show was the Golden Globes the year I was nominated for *Up in the Air*. When you're wearing a long dress, which I was for the first time, you want to go for height and comfort in your shoe choice. Style really doesn't matter because no one is ever going to see them. But as this was my first Golden Globes, I wanted to wear this perfect pair of punishing, embellished skyscrapers. They were ridiculously painful, but they were a work of art. Because I knew I wouldn't be able to endure an entire evening in them, my publicist put a pair of slightly less ridiculous shoes in her bag to hand off to me once I was done with the red carpet. After I walked the carpet and sat down in the ballroom, I ripped off the skyscrapers, but my feet were so swollen they wouldn't even fit into the "easy" shoes. I sat through the entire program with my bare feet under the table, praying that by the time the show was over I'd be able to squeeze them into my footwear. If I'd won, I would have looked like a little girl in her mother's dress, hobbling up onstage. But that was the year I met the voice of Dug, so the night was a win.

The first time I got to present was that same year at the SAG Awards. I was wearing a strapless purple gown and nervously fiddled with the bodice as I waited backstage. Eventually, Stanley Tucci, who was presenting with me, leaned in and said, "Stop adjusting your boobs, you look fine."

The award went to Drew Barrymore for *Grey Gardens*, and she gave a flustered but obviously heartfelt speech. We escorted her offstage, and once we were in the wings, we turned to congratulate her. She walked steadily past us, leaned against a pillar, and closed her eyes. She was holding her award low by her waist and breathing slowly in and out. I thought, *Something real is happening in front of me. This is a human, taking a moment for herself because everything else has been pageantry.*

Stanley and I backed up a bit more. A woman wearing a headset crept near her with a desperate look on her face, but Drew Barrymore, movie star and recent SAG Award recipient, was not ready to turn herself back on. The woman in the headset finally squeaked, "Miss Barrymore, we're just gonna take you back here to have some pictures—"

"Just give me a second." She was perfectly calm and perfectly polite, but she was serious.

"Can I get you some water?" (It never fails.)

"Sure."

The woman disappeared to get a glass of water. I suspect that this was more about buying time than being thirsty. Stanley and I stayed quiet and tiptoed past her. Just before she was out of view, I turned back to see her still standing there, eyes closed. I looked away quickly, because even observing her felt like an invasion. But it was sort of beautiful. She'd just been honored for a project she clearly cared about deeply and was resolved to experience that moment on her own terms.

The Oscars of a Parallel Universe

I had a very different experience presenting an award at the Oscars that year. At most award shows, you have the option to rehearse. At the Oscars, rehearsal is mandatory. It doesn't matter if you're Brad Pitt or screen legend Sidney Poitier, you come in the day before to walk the little path to your mark and say your intro into the microphone. It is "strongly recommended" that women rehearse in their heels.

I was paired with Zac Efron, and in my jeans and ridiculous shoes I asked him, "May I take your arm?" The rehearsal is filmed and treated as a full production so that the director, cameramen, and editors can root out any potential mishaps. There are hired stand-ins scattered in the audience, sitting in the seats of all the nominees.

We walked our path and said our lines and waited for the winner to be announced. For rehearsal, the winner is chosen completely at random, so the camera crew will be prepared for anything. I was presenting the award for Best Sound Editing and (as I'm sure you remember) Paul N. J. Ottosson won for *The Hurt Locker*. But in the rehearsal, *Inglourious Basterds* won. A gentleman from the audience stood up and made his way to the stage. I gave him a perfunctory embrace ('cause that's what you do) and backed up about four feet to the "listening" mark, where the presenter waits until the speech is over. Now, if I were this dude, I would just go, "Thank you, thank you, speech speech speech, I'm making my speech, it's going on for about sixty seconds, thank you so much, good night."

Instead, I was treated to a thoughtful monologue about the joys of working with Quentin Tarantino, the trials and triumphs of the sound-editing process, and the importance of family above all. I'd fallen into a parallel universe. This had taken research. He wasn't reading off of anything, which meant he had memorized all this information and all these names. I realized that something strange was happening in the audience. Even though these people were not involved in the nominated films, even though the winners were chosen completely at random, they must have been sitting there thinking, *Call my guy's name, come on, call my guy's name.* I do not know how the rehearsal nominees are hired, but the screening process seems to find people fitting the description "kooky but harmless . . . we hope."

The real deal was equally surprising. The presentation went smoothly, Mr. Ottosson accepted his award, and I escorted him offstage. The weird thing was what happened after. What's the first thing you would want to do after winning an Oscar? Jump into the arms of your loved ones and collaborators? Of course that's what you'd want! But that's not what happens. What happens is that the two goons you've never met before who just butchered the pronunciation of your name are whisked around with you to take a series of commemorative and candid photos in different setups around the theater.

First stop is the wings just offstage—*snap, snap, smile, how do you feel, congratulations.* Next is a long walk down a dim hallway to a professional-looking photo setup: all-white background, good lighting, pose with the presenters, pose by yourself (while the presenters get a drink)—*smile, do a serious one, hold out the Oscar, snap, snap, congratulations.* Last up, a door is opened to a small ballroom, and bleachers full of photographers start snapping and screaming. You know that scene in *Notting Hill* when Hugh Grant tries to tell Julia Roberts not to open the door (but somehow can't get out the words "Don't open the door." Come on, Richard Curtis, you're better than that!) and she opens the door and is confronted by a sea of flashing lights and demanding voices? It's like that. You walk onto a platform—*snap, snap, smile, over here, hold out the Oscar, snap, snap, congratulations, but I need you to look over here.* This room goes on the longest and is the most aggressive. Though, to be honest, I prefer the unbridled onslaught to the cordial desperation of the other stops. Then there are solo photos in the ballroom (again, the presenters go get a drink) and eventually you go back to your seat.

I've presented to groups before—sometimes the winner of a technical award will be a small team—and those seem less jarring. They can enjoy the win together and throw each other what-the-hell-is-happening looks, which must make it more manageable. But accepting an award by yourself has the hardest comedown I've ever witnessed.

One year after I presented an award, I was waiting in the hallway outside the auditorium to go back to my seat. You have to wait for a commercial break, so I was back there for a few minutes. Lupita Nyong'o walked up and stood across from me in the hall. She had, perhaps fifteen minutes prior, won an Oscar for *12 Years a Slave*.

"Congratulations," I said.

She smiled, gave me a nod, then looked back down at the award in her hands. *Jesus*, I thought, *Lupita Nyong'o just won an Academy Award for starring in her first film; her family, the cast and crew are mere feet beyond these doors, and she's gotta stare at my stupid mug for another three minutes before she can hug them? This is a travesty. Someone hand her a glass of champagne! Or a puppy! Or a male model to make out with!*

A similar thing happened at the Grammys. I was waiting to introduce a musical act and Sam Smith walked toward me after winning Best New Artist. He got to the bottom of the stairs under the stage and stopped. He looked around, Grammy in hand, and asked me in his sweet accent, "Do you know where I'm supposed to go?" *Travesty! Champagne! Puppy! Male model!*

I didn't know where he was supposed to go. I just stood there, a living reminder that even after you win a Grammy you've got to put up with idiots who don't know anything. I think Drew Barrymore had the right idea.

Most of All, I'd Like to Thank Cate Blanchett

The year I was nominated for *Up in the Air* was fun because I knew I wasn't going to win. I know that sounds like bullshit, and of course the best iteration of an award season would be to win everything and make yourself an impractical but fabulous head-dress with your many statuettes. However, that year, Mo'Nique won almost every award for the absolutely harrowing perfor-mance she gave in the film *Precious*. I won the National Board of Review, but in that instance the winner is announced before the ceremony.

There was never a "and the winner is" type show where I was going over a potential acceptance speech. I can't imagine the stress of a close call, hearing your name at some events and someone else's name at others. Doubly fun was that all of us in the *Up in the Air* gang were destined to be losers. George was up for Best Actor, which was always later in the program. After my category was presented, he would turn to me and whisper, "I'm still a nominee and you're just some loser." Knowing you weren't going to win wasn't what you wanted, but at least you could drink.

The only time I've been genuinely happy to lose an award was when I was nominated for an Independent Spirit Award for *Rocket Science*. I didn't stand a chance anyway (I was up against Cate Blanchett), but I wouldn't have been able to make a speech if I had won because—drumroll—I was high off my face.

The afternoon before the show, I'd felt a tingling sensation in my nose. Actually, it wasn't quite in my nose, it was behind my nose. By that night it had become painful, and in the mirror my face looked swollen and slightly warped. I thought maybe I was having an allergic reaction to something, but I didn't think allergies were so painful. Whatever was swelling in my nose was hard and it was putting pressure on the area above my lip, making it uncomfortable to smile. The ceremony was the next afternoon and I hoped that it would be gone when I woke up.

In the morning, it had gotten significantly worse and I walked across the apartment to wake my roommate Alex. I knocked on his door.

"You need to take me to the hospital."

He opened the door, half asleep. "You look weird."

We went to the emergency room and, much like my parents, no one there had ever heard of the Independent Spirit Awards. Where are the film fans in this town? They did not seem moved to bump me to the top of the ER's priority list. I sat in the waiting room staring at my face in the reflection of my smudged metal purse handle. Whatever was happening was painful, too painful to touch, but when I wrote nine out of ten on my form's pain scale, even the admissions nurse knew it was a lie. Somebody fix my face!! I had an award to lose!

After a while a doctor took me into a hospital room and told me I had an infection that had created a cyst inside my nose. *Charming.* It was minor, but still serious because of its proximity to my brain.

I chose this moment to say, "Have you ever heard of the Spirit Awards? They're like the Oscars of independent film."

He put his hand on my forehead for leverage.

"Stop talking, I have to lance it."

Lance, as in, cut open. That's right! The hard, unbearably tender thing behind my nose was about to be stabbed and drained. And the way in? Up my nostril! He told me he was going to numb it with something called "freezing spray" and proceeded to stick a nozzle into my nose and spray in a cold liquid. Funny thing about your nose, though: it rejects fluids being shot into it, because your brain thinks you're drowning. It's the same principle as waterboarding. I involuntarily pulled away several times and spluttered wildly when he held my head.

The doctor looked at me, as disappointed as he was frustrated, and eventually said, "Well, if that's the best we can do, this is going to hurt."

I didn't want to be stabbed in my still-throbbing nose, but at that point anything seemed like a better alternative to more freezing spray.

I was wrong.

You know when a doctor says "This is going to hurt" and they do whatever they have to do and you think, *This is un-fucking-believable I can't stand it fuck fuck fuck,* but you just sit there grimacing in silence? This was the only time I have shouted in front of a doctor. It was totally involuntary, and once it was over I was surprised to find tears had already reached my neck.

In terms of medical ailments, I count myself extremely lucky to have had something immediately treatable that had no long-term repercussions. But once he hooked me up to a drip of painkillers and the world came into logical (but loopy) focus, between the fact that I hadn't yet brushed my teeth, I wasn't wearing underwear, and pus was still draining from a cyst in my face, I abandoned any hope of making it to Santa Monica in time for an award show ninety minutes later.

Alex came into the room. I whimpered a little, both exhausted and stoned.

"Don't smile, you still look weird. Okay, see, when you're not smiling you look okay. I mean, you look like you're hungover, and you're very oily, but you don't look like you've been crying in a hospital bed." He threw my hoodie at me. "Let's go."

At least, that's what I think he said. I could be wrong because I was high as fuck. We got through the discharge paperwork as quickly as possible, and even though the sight of the bill made me want to flee the state and start a new life with the mole people, we raced home. In the car, my head bobbled back and forth, and I tried to say that we'd never make it.

Alex recoiled. "Your face looks weird when you talk, too, so don't do that either."

At home I brushed my teeth, put on underwear (I hope), and pulled on my dress. I put all the makeup I could find in a plastic bag and got back in his car. My eyes were still puffy, but I slapped on enough makeup to cover the dark circles. I hung my head out the window like a dog for the rest of the ride, trying to dry my sweaty hair and sober up.

I checked my face in the mirror again. "What do I do if people ask why I won't smile for a photo? Should I try to explain the nose thing? Should I say I had dental surgery? I'll say I had dental surgery."

"Anna, listen to me, because this is important: there is no version where you should say anything to anyone."

The next thing I remember is being pushed onto the carpet and hearing photographers shout, "Smile! Over here! Smile! What's her name? Smile! Sweetie, how do you spell your name? Smile!" I was passed off to Jeff Blitz, the director of *Rocket Science*, who got me to my seat and force-fed me bread and water.

For a moment I considered what to do if I won. *Would it be bad to mention it? Would it be worse to not mention it? Should I just hide my mouth by pressing myself too close to the microphone? Should I say I'm high? I'll say I'm high. Yeah, that'll be the best thing.*

Cate Blanchett won. Of all the amazing contributions that woman has made to the world, beating me that day is the thing I'm most grateful for.

Jeff leaned in to me and quietly joked, "I demand a recount!"

I slowly turned to face him.

"I'm tripping balls."

I stared at him for about twenty solid seconds, then turned back to the stage.

Here's a picture of my stoned face, so you don't have to Google it later.

Forty-five minutes after leaving
my hospital bed and looking fly.

Sometimes, the Shoe Flies Too Far

The year *Into the Woods* came out, I was asked to perform at the Oscars. I got a call from Neil Patrick Harris and producers Craig Zadan and Neil Meron. Actually, I got an email from my publicist saying Neil and the producers wanted to set up a call; we arranged a time over a series of emails and eventually called in using a conference service. It was so unexpected!

I'm sure most people know this, but for those of you who missed the broadcast because of a family emergency or a Chilean coal mine–type situation, I was asked to be part of the opening number, in which Neil professes his love for movies while a series of famous film clips play behind him. The final clip would be Cinderella running down the steps of the palace, and I was to appear onstage, as if I'd burst out of the screen. Neil and I would sing for a while and be "rudely" interrupted by a curmudgeon in the form of the hilarious Jack Black.

I was over the moon about all this. They asked me if I would have a problem performing *as* Cinderella, and not as myself. If they'd asked me to perform a one-woman *Puppetry of the Penis*, I would have figured it out. I was beyond excited. An announcement was made, I started learning my music, I dusted off my Spanx. Then I got the following email from one Mr. Ben Affleck:

They want me to present at the Oscars, but we have this insane 3:30 a.m. call. So I couldn't make it back. I read you are performing? How are you making it work?

Ben and I were in the middle of shooting *The Accountant* in Atlanta, and this email sent a hot spike down my back.

I frantically called my agent.

"Hey, so I just got an email from Ben and he's saying that they won't let him out of this crazy call time the day after the

Oscars and it's a scene that we're both in and I assumed that I didn't have a work conflict and I'm freaking out!"

He told me to calm down, he told me it would work out. I suspect that when he hung up the phone he threw up.

All I can say is god bless Ben Affleck. Once both of us were potentially going to be part of the broadcast, Warner Brothers agreed that to make it work, they would hire a private jet (!) to take us from LA to Atlanta immediately following the ceremony. Player WHAA—I can't pull that off—I was super stoked.

The unglamorous reality of this situation was that in the back of the car that took me to the Academy Awards was a suitcase packed with a travel toothbrush, cotton socks and underwear, an old rain jacket (Atlanta was due for a storm), my laptop, and a week's supply of sweatpants, a.k.a. two pairs of sweatpants.

My dress that year was a custom peach gown. It was temporarily constructed with a thin cord that tied the neckline of the dress together, but was designed to incorporate a diamond collar necklace. Having a diamond necklace hold up your dress is nerve-wracking but sexy as fuck, and I would give the experience a ten out of ten. However, just to make sure that nothing malfunctioned, once the dress was on me, my stylist had to sew it to the necklace. This process was about fifteen minutes of being occasionally pricked by a needle with my head tilted awkwardly to one side. Still sexy, still loving it. Being sewn into a diamond necklace is not a thing you are allowed to be annoyed over in real life.

I arrived early since I was in the opening number and had to change clothes. The red carpet can get hectic as showtime approaches, but having a reason to be there before the rush meant there were fewer bodies and less stress. It was almost relaxing, but eerie, like being in a slaughterhouse before the cattle are brought in. I walked the carpet in my pretty, flowing gown. I was very happy to be out of the crash position, and nothing malfunctioned, so I went backstage to change. My stylist met me in my dressing room and slowly cut me out of my dress and necklace. Still sexy, still loving it.

I got into my Cinderella costume, had a quick hair change, and started warming up. I could hear Adam Levine and John Legend warming up in the echoey halls, and I wondered what the hell I thought I was doing. But Jack Black was in the room next door and he started a casual conversation through the thin wall. We lobbed jokes back and forth, which calmed my nerves. Jack may share the Clooney gene for spotting and preventing a potential downward spiral.

I stood backstage and waited for my cue. I would put this moment in the top three scariest of my life. Even writing about it makes me queasy. The number of my heroes sitting in the Dolby on Oscar night was almost comical. I wasn't worried about the millions of people watching at home; I was afraid I was going to fall on my ass in front of Oprah.

My cue came and I ran onstage. I sang my first line to the audience and got entrance applause—entrance applause, motherfucker! Hot crowd, I love it! Then I turned to sing my second line to Neil. Lovely Neil. Seeing him made my anxiety drop. No matter what happened, having this guy as a parachute meant we'd be fine. We sang our silly bits to each other, and then Jack Black came on and absolutely destroyed the place.

The hard part was over for me by this point and I got to fully enjoy his amazing comedic and vocal stylings. My last bit was a gag where I scream at Jack to "Beat it!" and throw Cinderella's slipper after him as he exits.

In rehearsals, the problem was often that I didn't throw the shoe far enough and it was unclear that Jack was being attacked. Performance adrenaline led to an overcorrection, and I threw the shoe clear offstage. Neil and I couldn't tell if it was offstage from where we were, but we were nervous. The next piece was supposed to be Neil walking to my shoe, picking it up, and handing it back to me. The music started up again and Neil headed toward the opposite side of the stage, scanned the ground, and turned back in a graceful loop. Lovely, consummately professional, Neil skated back to me and took both my hands and looked into my eyes like, *I guess you're exiting half barefoot, sugar.* We took our final breath as song partners and I was on my way offstage. Hopefully, no one knew that wasn't the plan.

I walked to my dressing room in a haze trailed by a wardrobe girl and a few stage managers, got out of my Cinderella costume, sat down in my underwear, and had a drink. Finally I squeaked, "The shoe wasn't supposed to go offstage."

A chorus of people assured me they hadn't noticed anything wrong, and I believed them, because what else was I going to do?

I got back into my peach dress and, once again, my stylist sewed me into the necklace. Still sexy, still loving it. Or at least, *liking* it very much and feeling very appreciative for this moment in my life. I had another drink and got ready to present an award with Kevin Hart. I asked him, "May I take your arm?" and we walked onstage.

I was allowed to stay until Ben presented his award since the plane couldn't take off without him. I sat in the audience and watched Lady Gaga perform. Her seats were right next to mine, but while she was onstage her parents moved up and sat in them to watch her. I imagine that Lady Gaga has done a lot of things that confuse her parents, no matter how supportive they may be. Watching Lady Gaga's *parents* watch Lady Gaga nail a musical tribute to Julie Andrews was extraordinary. When Ms. Andrews herself joined their daughter onstage, their pride almost took solid form next to me.

The last thing I got to see was John Legend and Common perform "Glory." I had seen them perform it at the Grammys earlier that month (yeah, guess what, I'm a big deal) but something special was happening in the auditorium that night. Maybe it was having their cast and crew there, maybe Oprah really does make every room more magical. Chris Pine's single tear was no bullshit.

Just before Ben presented his award, I slipped out and headed to the pickup point. I had to walk back through the red carpet, this time jarringly empty. I got in the car and headed straight to the airport. It didn't matter if the dress got wrinkled now, so I could bend at the waist like a normal human and the ride was very comfortable.

We pulled up in front of a private plane on a deserted, pitch-black tarmac. I stepped out of my car and thought, *This is the most unreal situation I've ever been in and I'm getting a damn picture of it.* Still in the gown and the diamond necklace, I asked the pilot to take my photo on the steps of the plane. Does taking photos in these situations negate your ability to seem cool in them? You bet your ass it does. But COME ON. This was impossibly swanky and no one else was around. I gave the pilot my best sheepish, apologetic smile and got on the plane.

"Hey, what took you so long?" Ben and his assistant had beat me there. "You're doing a photo shoot out there now? We've got places to be."

They'd both already changed into jeans and T-shirts. *How*, I ask you, *how?*

I never posted my photo anywhere because it felt too douchey, but we're friends now, so you guys know I'm super down to earth. Please ignore my previous comment about being a big deal.

Everyone got ready to take off and I grabbed my sweats and

a hoodie and headed toward the bathroom. I pulled the flight attendant aside and produced a small nail file.

"Hi, I'm Anna, it's nice to meet you. I'm sorry to do this to you when we've just met, but I'm going to need you to cut me out of this dress."

scrappy
little
nobody

my grandmother's funeral

I think of my mom as a softie. She emotes more than anyone else in the family. She has a big, easy smile, and most of my friends describe her as "adorable" within three minutes of knowing her. She's a people pleaser, but she doesn't take shit from anybody.

When I was in the second week of filming *Pitch Perfect* in Baton Rouge, my mother called me around five a.m. to tell me that my grandmother had died. She was ninety-three. The woman had made miraculous recoveries from illness and injury, but she'd said for years that she was ready to die, and a few weeks after asking express permission from both of her daughters, she let go.

My mom didn't cry. Sometimes I forget that when it comes to serious matters, she's kind of stoic and dignified. If she didn't object to violence, she would have made an impressive and beloved general.

I didn't cry either. The funeral plans would be made soon; she needed to discuss them with the rest of the family. We said good-bye and I got ready for work. It was Monday, which meant an early call time, so I needed to be out the door soon anyway.

I stopped at base camp to tell Debbie, our makeup artist. Actors have weird interactions with the vanity departments. We tell them private things like "I think I'm getting a rash" or "I'm on my period," the way a race car driver would tell his pit crew that the wheel's pulling a little to the left. Sometimes, we have to tell them that a family member has died.

I stepped up into the trailer and very quickly said, "Hey, Debbie, I'm fine, but I wanted to let you know my grandmother passed this morning, so you may have to keep an eye on me."

I've always appreciated when someone can sense that I am trying to keep it together and they don't show too much sympathy.

"I'm so sorry to hear that. I'll have you covered." She put a tube of waterproof mascara on her station and gave me a nod.

Next, I had to go to set to tell Tommy, our second assistant director. When you start making movies, nobody tells you who to inform in the event of a death, but the second AD is an information hub, and I liked Tommy, so I decided on him. I rode to our shooting location in a van with a bunch of the cast. The small blessing of a five a.m. call time is that no one wants to talk. I did wonder if wearing my sunglasses pre-sunrise made me look more closed off than usual, but I also didn't really care.

I found Tommy, and I don't remember what I said, but I found myself crying hard almost immediately. I was caught off guard; I really thought I'd be able to tell him without breaking. I was choking through "Sorry, shit, I'm sorry, Jesus, I thought I could stay professional and just tell you and I'm really sorry."

I felt like I was letting my mom down. I'd made it through that conversation with some dignity, and here I was crying in front of Tommy, making him embarrassed and uncomfortable. He was very kind of course, and he didn't offer me water, which I respected. He told me he'd let "them" know and went off to speak to whoever "they" are.

The truth is, I didn't know what happened in these situations. I'd never wanted to ask, because asking would acknowledge that something bad might happen during a shoot.

Luckily, later that day my mom told me the family could have the service on Saturday. When I updated Tommy he looked relieved. So I still don't know what happens if your family can't have a funeral on your day off, and I've still never asked.

When I walked away from Tommy after that first conversation, Jinhee Joung, the actress who played Kimmy Jin, my character's apathetic roommate, introduced herself. It was her first day and she wanted to say hi. I still had my sunglasses on and I was acting incredibly distant. I've always wondered if she thought I was a bitch or if she could tell I'd been crying, but I never explained myself. Maybe she just thought I was tired. Either way, her dry humor made me think that perhaps, like me, she didn't put a lot of stock in "nice" anyway.

We were getting ready to shoot the activities fair scene, and once the sun came up, I was happy to be spending the day outside. One by one, all the producers came up and said something awkward to me. Obviously, they had the best intentions and it's the Emily Post thing to do, and I'm the weird one for hating it so much, but I wished more people could tell the difference between the "leave me alone" vibe I give off all the time by accident and my actual "leave me alone" vibe.

I wasn't sure if people in the cast would find out, and I wasn't sure I wanted them to. I didn't want anyone to think I was irritated with them, but at the same time I didn't want to field more perfunctory condolences. But perhaps because death isn't juicy gossip, or because everyone was used to me being a misanthrope, or because by noon that day Kim Kardashian had announced she was divorcing Kris Humphries after just seventy-two days of marriage, my news had not spread.

After lunch our director, Jason Moore, was going over an upcoming shot with me. Because it was a Steadicam shot, for a moment we found ourselves alone in a crowd. We were both idly studying the prop flyers on the "activity booth" in front of us, and he took a breath. "Hey, I didn't say anything before—"

"Huh-uh."

By the time I hit the second syllable he was walking away. He really sees me. About a month later he brought it up again and we said a few sentences about it. That was it.

We shot more of the activities fair the next day, and on Wednesday we switched to nights to shoot the "riff-off." Thursday was more of the riff-off and Friday we shot the initiation party scene where Jesse tells Beca they are going to have aca-children and Chloe gives her some bi-curious vibes. Not a bad night for Beca, actually. It was a little trickier for me. Night shoots start at sundown and go until sunrise, so we were scheduled to finish that scene around seven a.m. Saturday morning, the morning of the funeral. My flight was at seven a.m., so I packed my suitcase and brought it to set with me and got in a van to the airport at five a.m. That wide shot of us all dancing at the end of that scene? I'm not in it.

I got through airport security and took off my makeup with a wet wipe in the bathroom. The sun started to rise. Since there are no direct flights from Baton Rouge to Bradenton, Florida, where my family was, my first leg took me somewhere in Texas. I understood that this was my fastest option, but as the fatigue started to set in, it was maddening to know that I was heading farther from my destination. The ability to sleep on planes would have been helpful. The next leg took me to Florida and I landed midday.

My mom picked me up at the airport and we headed straight to the funeral home. I changed in the car so we wouldn't be late. I had borrowed a simple dress from the *Pitch Perfect* wardrobe department since I didn't have anything in Baton Rouge that was appropriate for a funeral.

The service was lovely. Either the elderly are practiced at giving compliments or people really loved my grandmother. She may have been insensitive about weight gain and curt about proper piecrust technique and used terms like "lifestyle choice," but she was generous to a fault and put others before herself. You could feel the love in the room. My mom started to lose it and so did I. Five years earlier, I'd refused to cry at my grandfather's funeral as part of some misguided point of pride. My brother had done a reading and after every line, I distracted myself by making up a Dr. Seuss–like rhyme in my head.

"He will not be burned though through the fire he walks."

I would not, could not with a fox!

Even though I was exhausted, that wasn't the reason I couldn't hold it together this time. My mom was grieving the loss of her mother. I knew that before, but I could feel it now, and seeing my mom in that kind of pain was simply awful.

I'd never been in a receiving line before, but everyone had nice things to say or a story to share. A few people seemed too happy to meet me given the circumstances. Some told me how proud my grandma was of me, and my mom would chime in, even through tears, "She was proud of all her grandchildren." That was true. She talked about all four of us constantly; certain people just had selective interests. A few mourners seemed more focused on making weird comments to me than on grieving, which pissed me off, but I tried to grimace through it and chalk it up to faulty social filters after seventy or something.

Then, as my mother stood next to me weeping, a woman reached for my hand and smiled as though she was about to say something playful and a little bit naughty.

"So you're the actress! Oh, you're very good . . . but we know these aren't acting tears!"

Lady, what the fuck did you just say to me? You mean the tears streaming down my face as we prepare to bury my grandmother and my own mother sobs next to me? No, these are not "acting tears."

Maybe she says weird shit in every situation, maybe she felt like a jerk about it afterward, but I've never come so close to hitting someone who was smiling in my face.

I had to get to Vancouver, because I was shooting a scene in *The Company You Keep* the next morning. Oh yeah, that was happening, too. I'd been warned that the logistics would be tricky because of *Pitch Perfect*, but I had said yes because Robert Redford was directing and that seemed like a once-in-a-lifetime kind of thing.

Under the circumstances, leaving my mother to film a glorified cameo felt decidedly unimportant. There was already a car in the parking lot waiting to take me to the airport. The situation was not conducive to grief. I said good-bye to my relatives and got my suitcase out of my mom's trunk. In the car I changed back into jeans and browsed Reddit on my phone. I bought some trail mix at the airport and got on a plane to my layover city.

When I arrived in Seattle I saw my final leg into Vancouver was delayed. I found an empty corner of the airport—it wasn't hard because at this point it was almost ten p.m.—and I sat still without any technology. I really cried for her then. Before, I had cried from discomfort and I had cried for my mom, but now, in an empty row of airport seating, I thought about my grandma. I'd be lying if I said we were extremely close. Both of my older cousins had spent more time with her as they grew up and I was envious of the relationship they had. But she had bathed me in her sink, and taught me to read, and she'd been a moral standard my whole life. She was a devout woman, and even though I am not, I fully expect that she is in the illustrated children's Bible version of heaven. If she was on some plane now where she could see my soul laid bare, I wondered if she would be proud of me.

I got on my flight to Vancouver.

We landed, I got my work permit, made it through customs, and checked into my hotel. I'd been awake for thirty-two hours, but I still ordered a burger and a vodka, 'cause sometimes you can't call it a day until something good happens.

The next day, Sunday, I filmed a scene with Shia LaBeouf and Terrence Howard. Those actors have reputations for being . . . eccentric, but both of them were sensitive, warm, and professional, which I needed more than they could have known. But in retrospect it's kind of a disappointment.

Mr. Redford was equally lovely. In one shot at the end of the night my character is looking at an image of Redford as a young man. In between takes, he came up behind me, looked at the photo, sighed wistfully, and said, "God, I had fun."

My stomach flipped and I hoped that if my grandmother was hanging out in my soul, she got a kick out of that.

That night I showered and got on a plane back to the *Pitch Perfect* set. When we touched down in Baton Rouge, it was Monday morning. I don't actually remember if I went to my room and showered before going to set . . . I hope for the sake of my coworkers I had time. We were filming the finale performance and I was glad to have something physical to focus on. Some of the cast asked me how the Redford thing went, but it seemed most did not know anything else had happened.

Working regularly has only made it harder to get home. Even when I'm not shooting, I have so many side projects that I have to check with five different "departments" in my life to ask permission to visit.

Sometimes I fantasize about leaving LA and living on a little boat off the coast of Maine so I could see my family whenever I want. I doubt my hectic brain would let me do that. Plus I don't think Seamless does maritime deliveries.

I used to joke about turning down certain movies that had explicit content because "my grandmother's alive and I'd like to keep it that way." I thought about it as we continued to film the movie. It was only a joke, of course, but the day I shouted, "THAT'S MY DICK," I thought it was probably for the best that my grandma would never see *Pitch Perfect*.

fake parties i have planned
with the detail of a real party

Now that I am doing my dream job, I fantasize about a social life. I know what you're thinking: *But Anna, everything you've said in this book makes you sound so fun to be around! You must have literally thousands of friends at your beck and call!*

Sadly, even if that were true (it is—I am very well-liked, and anyone who tells you otherwise is just frightened by the power of their love for me), I barely have time to see anyone. Usually when I *am* at home, I've just come back from months out of town and I only have the energy to pick various essentials out of my oversize luggage day by day, leaving a trail of laundry, heat-styling tools, and half-empty bottles of face wash in every room. But even though my place is in a perpetual state of squalor, and I've got a maximum of three solid relationships in my life at any given moment, I've always dreamed of being a world-class hostess. I'm talking about chic-ass, highly detailed, "Suck on *that*, Pinterest"–style parties. These are just a few of the classy imaginary bashes I've thrown.

Christmas

Christmas is the ultimate party opportunity. It's the only holiday that has whole categories of food, alcohol, and music dedicated to it. The décor can be elegant and traditional, modern and monochromatic, or whimsical and eclectic. If I could have my house decorated for Christmas year-round, I'd do it. In fact, if I could have nothing in my house BUT Christmas décor, that would be ideal. Seriously, if it were up to me, I wouldn't even have furniture. Wait, it IS up to me? Oh crap.

So I'm really not interested in interior design beyond tiny lights and tacky snow globes. One day I might start faking a romantic madness like a rich spinster in a Victorian novel so I can live in a winter wonderland full-time. I hate Christmas itself—it's nothing but a source of anxiety and disappointment—but, like getting naked with a hot guy, I like the *idea* of it.

My house is on a narrow, winding street off several other narrow, winding streets. It's hard to find and parking is minimal. My neighbors are also so mean about parking that when I moved in, I thought they were doing a comedy bit. I playfully yelled back at them until the day I realized they legit hated me. This makes it complicated to throw my ultimate (imaginary) Christmas soiree, but I have a festive solution. I rent out a parking lot at the bottom of the hill and hire a team of drivers for the evening.

Did I mention that I spare no expense on my imaginary parties? Guests drop off their vehicles in the lot and get in one of a small fleet of town cars waiting to take them to my front door. Not only is preselected Christmas music playing in the car, but the interior is decorated to the nines. Lit garland along the windows, red velvet across the seats, tiny dishes of potpourri in the cup holders. The drivers will have a simple sprig of holly in their lapels. No Santa hats. A grown man in a Santa hat always looks like a dog in a sweater: they might put up with it, but you can tell they hate you for it.

The outside of my house would put the Griswolds' to shame. The very nature of light-up outdoor décor is garish, so I support going all out. I've even got a Santa on the roof and a bunch of those animatronic reindeer on the front lawn. Fuck the environment, it's Christmas! To get through the door, guests have to sing their favorite Christmas carol—just the first line, I'm not a monster—and then they are presented with an assortment of holiday beverage options: wassail (a.k.a. hot cider with booze), mulled wine, or eggnog with spiced rum. Served on a silver filigree platter by an attractive waiter, natch.

The inside of my place would be *decked out*. And not just the living room. Every inch of my house would look like a Christmas-themed playland. I've always hated that moment at holiday parties when you catch a glimpse into some nautical-inspired guest room and remember that Christmas is a farce designed to distract us from the existential dread and monotony of our pathetic, meaningless lives and—*Goooood King Wenceslas looked out! On the Feast of Stephen!*

But that won't happen at my party! Anyone could walk into any room to "put down their coat" or "snoop through my shit" (Nice try, suckers! I buried everything embarrassing in the backyard in preparation for this party!) without breaking the holiday spirit.

The food would be inspired by *Game of Thrones*. Did you know there are websites dedicated to creating recipes inspired by the dishes described in the books and on the show? Obviously, I've hired someone who runs a *GoT* food site to cater. I'm too busy sexually harassing the waiters to cook anything myself. (Don't worry, they all find me charming, not lecherous and entitled. No, really! It's like how every guy I know has told me a story about going to Hooters and how the waitress seemed "grateful" to finally have a customer who was "cool and fun." Definitely not bullshit!)

There's a game of Yankee Swap with gag gifts once everyone is drunk enough to think a Shake Weight is hilarious. Then a Will Ferrell impersonator performs a scene from *Elf* once everyone is drunk enough to think it's actually Will Ferrell. Even though it's my fantasy, I don't like the idea that the real Will Ferrell would be willing to come to some jerk's Christmas party for money.

Everyone gets sent home with a gift bag of candy, the Michael Bublé holiday album, and a very tasteful, very delicate gold necklace in a box buried at the bottom, so they won't discover it until they get home and then they'll think what a thoughtful, generous friend I am. Is it extravagant? Yes. But it's my imaginary money and I'll spend it how I please. Since everyone's hammered, the drivers take the guests home safely and work in teams through the night to return their cars by morning. There's a thank-you note on the windshield, because I have thought of EVERYTHING.

Valentine's Day

I think the "single gals," "anti–Valentine's Day" thing is a little played out. The romantic Valentine's thing is a little played out, too. I also know that every dude thinks this holiday is a trap; your lady says she doesn't want to exchange gifts or do anything special, but secretly she wants you to surprise her with something anyway. (I don't think ladies actually trap men like this, but if you are a lady who does: cut it out, you're proving those boring dudes right.)

Perhaps a Valentine's Day party should be left to someone better versed in romance. I'm sort of "the cooler" when it comes to hooking up. I don't want you to think I'm not fun, I'm just the kind of gal who will find a book of anonymous World War I letters at a house party and sneak away from my crush to read them. Half an hour later he will find me weeping. He'll tell me to rejoin the party and I'll reply: "But it's all just so *sad*."

I think about that book more often than I think about that boy.

Nevertheless, I have a potential V-Day party plan. My imaginary Valentine's Day party is a mock restaurant at my house. I cook a little something, dim the lights, and arrange some candles. It's not like you can get a reservation anywhere else, so just come over, have a seat at a hastily decorated folding table, and don't complain about the food, because the chef will spit in your dessert. Couples, singles, gay, straight, cats, dogs, and well-trained lizards are welcome. No babies. If everyone feels like finishing the evening with an orgy, all the better.

St. Patrick's Day

I grew up in a mostly Irish community and everyone took their heritage pretty seriously. I was plain shocked when I came to LA and found people treating St. Patrick's Day like a Kermit-colored Mardi Gras.

My St. Patrick's Day party would take authentic Celtic inspiration—none of this neon-green tomfoolery. Guests are required to wear an Aran Island cable knit, and they will be provided a flat cap and a wooden pipe at the door. A bartender will be present, but only to continually dry the inside of a glass with a rag and supportively nod his head. The beer will be self-serve (and brown, thank you very much—green beer looks like radioactive piss) and the food will be Italian, not Irish, because I don't hate my friends.

If I invite family I'll have to hide anything that looks valuable. They wouldn't steal anything, but they would certainly get drunk and start throwing around terms like "hoity-toity" and asking if I thought I was better than them.

A confession booth will be available, but I'll find some Unitarian minister and (s)he'll hand out absolution like it's flavored vodka at an Iggy Azalea album release party. It won't get you into heaven, but it'll be over quickly. Public urination will be acceptable, dirty limericks will receive much bigger laughs than they deserve, and no one can talk about their feelings until they're blind drunk.

The party game will be a snake piñata to commemorate Saint Patrick driving the snakes out of Ireland. Yes, I know he didn't actually do that and that the snakes are druids or pagans or whatever and it's all some big allegory JUST HIT THE PIÑATA, ALL RIGHT?! YOU THINK YOU'RE BETTAH THAN ME?!

New Year's Eve

New Year's Eve is the holiday that needs an "anti" party. Girls started doing anti-Valentine's in protest of the outlandish expectations of that day, but for my money, NYE is the worst of the high-pressure, forced-fun offenders. Plus, champagne is the devil's work and even the expensive stuff makes me weepy and bloated.

This imaginary event is not catered, valeted, or overly planned. Come over in sweats and slippers. If you don't have any, I can provide them, not because I bought them in preparation, but because I love sweats and slippers and I happen to own enough to outfit a small, very comfortable army. No makeup, no champagne, no "You're leaving already?" good-bye guilt, and absolutely NO glitter. There will be Jenga, jigsaw puzzles, wine, whatever I have in my fridge (condiments and an empty Brita), maybe a stand-up special on Netflix, and hopefully some decent gossip about whoever didn't make it. I don't know what we'll do at midnight, because there will be no countdown. And if you're cool with me falling asleep mid-party, you can stay as long as you want.

Thanksgiving

I adore an "Orphans' Thanksgiving." I love my family, but Thanksgiving with friends feels awesome because I grew up watching TV shows about people who seemed to have no connections outside of their friend group, office, or community college.

The magic comes from the "playing house" quality that makes you feel more grown-up and more childlike simultaneously.

In my dream version the menu is as follows:

Dinner

Individual Cranberry Baked Brie Puff Pastries

Brussels Sprouts with Caramelized Onions and Crispy Bacon

Fried Mac-and-Cheese Balls with Truffle Oil

Buttery Jalapeño Cornbread

Lobster Mashed Potatoes

Garlic-and-Herb-Stuffed Mushrooms

Roasted Butternut Squash with Maple-Glazed Pecans

Prosciutto-Wrapped Asparagus Spears

Cranberry Sauce Out of the Can

Turkey, I Guess

Desserts

Pumpkin Crème Brûlée

Pumpkin Cake with Honey Cream Cheese Frosting

Pumpkin Cheesecake Bars

Pumpkin Whoopie Pies

Pumpkin Swiss Roll
Pumpkin Pie

I will defend pumpkin until the day I die. It's delicious. It's healthy. I don't understand the backlash. How did pumpkin become this embarrassing thing to love but bacon is still the cool flavor to add to everything? I don't have anything against bacon; just don't come after pumpkin like it's a crime to love an American staple.

Activities will include pretending to help in the kitchen, watching the Macy's Thanksgiving Day Parade, and saying you're so full you're going to throw up, then waiting ten minutes and getting more pie.

Once the sun has been down for a couple hours the Christmas season is technically upon us and it's time for the first Harry Potter marathon of the year, starting with film number three (because, obviously) and ending with film five, when the filthy casuals are allowed to go home. The hard-cores can sleep at my place and in the morning we will finish films six, seven, and seven-but-where-stuff-happens. Pumpkin pie for breakfast.

batten down the hatches

My friend Whitney is obsessed with the ocean. She decorates her Christmas tree with seashells and starfish and says things like, "Logically I know they're not, but I just *feel* like mermaids are real." Whitney invites me sailing shortly after I turn twenty-one. She and her family make an annual trip to Catalina, a truly tiny island off the coast of California, for an event called Buccaneer Days.

I've heard Whitney talk about this event before—it will be Alex's second time going—but I still don't understand what it is. Is it a costume contest? Is it a boat race? "It's an excuse for people to dress up and drink all day," she says.

Every year for a three-day weekend, Catalina plays host to about five hundred people (in about one hundred boats) who dress in elaborate pirate costumes, fly skull-and-crossbones flags, and refer to every beverage they consume as "grog."

To participate in Buccaneer Days, you sail to a port on Catalina called Two Harbors. You can spend the days on land or sea, and you sleep on your boat, tied to a mooring about a hundred yards from shore. Unlike Avalon—the adorable tourist town on the far side of the island—Two Harbors is not a community. There are no structures to sleep in, only a flimsy outdoor bar (because you don't need a roof, but you do need beer). The moorings in Two Harbors are limited and there's a wait list to lease one. Apparently applicants can wait thirty years for a spot. It's all very exclusive and old money. Whitney and her family strike me as far too normal to enjoy this kind of thing, but I'm grateful I've been invited along to witness the mayhem.

On the day we leave, Alex and I are still confused about the concept as a whole, but very excited. We scour our closets for anything on theme, pick out every article of clothing with so much as a ruffle on it, and stuff it into a bag. We stop at CVS to pick up a bandanna and an eye patch each. Neither of us has problems with motion sickness, but we grab some Ginger Trips, a holistic alternative to Dramamine, just to be safe. Upon inspection, the eye patches are a light gray, which makes them look distinctly medical and sad, so we toss them out. But we throw on our bandannas and take our Ginger Trips and drive to Long Beach.

We arrive at the marina and spot our hosts, looking spectacularly nautical. (I would describe the size and style of our vessel, but I don't know anything about sailing, so I'm trusting you to picture a boat.) The rest of the party is already onboard: Whitney and her new husband, Brian, and her childhood friends Katie and Cecily. Whitney's father tells me his name but I forget it immediately and hope that referring to him as "Captain" for the rest of the trip will be endearing. Then Whitney introduces me to her brother. Oh, unrelated: You know that thing when you meet someone and you're immediately like, *Huh. We're totally gonna have sex*—anyway, his name is Luke.

We throw our bags belowdecks and get settled into a cozy little section of the cockpit to enjoy the fresh air. Being from Maine and not knowing how to sail is one of those things that earns me lots of incredulous looks. Yet being *from* Maine is not the same as being someone who *summers* in Maine—so I don't want to ask too many questions right away. Whitney's father does appear to be the captain of the ship, and I surmise that Luke is a kind of default first mate. Oh, crafts this size don't have a first mate? Cool, I'm gonna call him that anyway so us poor kids can keep following along.

The Captain is having a conversation with someone on the dock about high winds. It sounds ominous, but we are so excited to take our trip that we choose to interpret the phrase "not quite gale force" as a green light. The family—except for Whitney's husband, Brian, who is on the bow reenacting scenes from *What About Bob?*—finishes readying the boat, while the passengers with no sailing experience chat and pass around a bag of chips. Luke is fiddling with something just behind me and leans down to whisper in my ear.

"Listen, I'm sure those chips are delicious, but this weekend you're the only girl I'm gonna see in a bikini that I haven't known since I was five. I'm counting on you."

This is presumptuous and rude, but I am twenty-one, so instead of jamming my keys through his calf, I find him incredibly charming. I make a big show of eating another handful of chips, then put the bag away and resolve to restrict myself to alcohol-based calories for the remainder of the trip.

We get out on the water and it is beautiful, but we are met with high winds as previously threatened. We try to take photos but most of them are blurred as the boat is tossed from side to side. The water is so choppy that a cooler of beer falls overboard and Luke leaps to action. He jumps into the dinghy and goes after the cooler. Everyone onboard watches with bated breath as he rescues the cooler and a couple runaway beers. He lifts the final can of PBR over his head and we cheer from the deck for our returning hero. I have a couple blurry photos of this, and that's where my pictures from this day stop.

Once Luke and the cooler are safely back onboard, the wind gets progressively worse. The boat is being thrown more than tossed now. We get past the breakwater, and I don't know it yet, but that means shit is about to go down. We take our electronics belowdecks and wrap ourselves in sweatshirts and jackets. Luke trims the sails—which is a thing you do on a boat—but it doesn't feel like it's made a difference. The conditions are a little distressing now and we look at each other with goofy, surprised expressions, the way you do when an elevator jolts. It's scary but it's fun and we can already imagine ourselves telling the story later. We make roller-coaster noises to confirm that *yes, this is fun, we're having fun.*

The water gets rougher and starts crashing over the sides of the boat. I'm worried about my hair getting wet and having that "attacked by a raccoon" look in front of this new boy, but I don't want to seem high maintenance at a time like this. The swells only get higher, and soon what's coming over us isn't foamy spray but thick sheets of blue water. I want to ask if this is normal, but I don't dare. I'm afraid of drowning but more afraid of looking ignorant and hysterical. Now that we are wet, I am unbearably cold. I go belowdecks to change, and maybe to do the cowardly thing and stay down there for a while. Turns out the feeling of motion sickness is fifty times worse belowdecks, and I run back up, still in my soaked hoodie. *That's fine*, I think, *better to be up here anyway. Solidarity and all that.*

The wind gets worse. No one is joking or making roller-coaster noises anymore. In fact we can't remember how we could ever have been so cavalier about the sea. The Captain is at the helm with a tight smile, reassuring us that he's not worried; he's seen worse. Luke is crouched down, bracing himself. He looks serious and ready for a fight. The rest of us are stone-faced, white-knuckling anything that's nailed down, as wave after wave comes over the boat. Then, before I even realize it's happening, I am throwing up.

I manage to thrust my body toward the side of the boat but I'm still clinging to the center of the cockpit with one hand, so my breakfast, the handful of chips, and the hippie Dramamine go all over the deck. I stay in my awkward position, not wanting to face the group of seasoned sailors. I know that under the circumstances no one will be angry, but I'm still humiliated. With waves coming over us at ten-second intervals, the evidence is washed away almost immediately, but I still don't turn around. *I am a pathetic, weak-stomached crybaby and I've never been so embarrassed.*

Then, before I even realize it's happening, Luke is throwing up beside me. For one moment I am relieved but it is short-lived. The first mate is violently throwing up next to me. This is a terrifying development. *I'm a girl about to die on a boat, who just moments ago was a girl embarrassed about throwing up on a boat.* I long for that simpler time.

I turn back to the Captain. He is no longer smiling.

Whitney throws up. Brian throws up. Cecily goes belowdecks to throw up. She returns cradling her cell phone to her ear, risking its destruction to call her fiancé and say "I love you." I think about the last time I had to swim hard, but I've lived in LA for years, where no one actually goes to the beach unless they're staging a romantic paparazzi shot to dispel gay rumors. It's been a very long time. I throw up again.

Who had we been an hour before? Who were those goons laughing and joking about the high waves? How could we have ever been so arrogant in the face of this inexhaustible power? We must be nearly there, we must be.

I still feel sick so I try to focus my gaze on a fixed landmark. I look back toward the California mainland but it's nowhere to be seen. I notice the Captain's galoshes are full to the brim with seawater, dark liquid splashing over the tops as we lurch. I stare at his overflowing boots while we hear mayday calls come over the radio. I don't care about my hair anymore.

The journey goes on and on, and just as Whitney starts apologizing to us, the waves start to get smaller. The Captain puts his tight smile back on to tell us it's getting better and he was never worried; he'd been through worse before anyway.

When we see land we behave like children who just found out the neighbor's scary dog is chained to a pole. Take THAT, ocean! You can't get us now! With no immediate threat to my life, I remember that I am in the presence of a hot guy and deflate a little knowing that I look like a drowned rat and probably blew it when I threw up the second time anyway.

The weather lets up completely by the time we get tied to our mooring. We take the dinghy to shore and dramatically kiss the ground because we think we're funny. There are little campground-style showers, where we get cleaned up and I do my best to fix my hair. Without a blow dryer, braided pigtails are my only style option. If pigtails could become a really fashionable look for adult women, that would make my life so much easier. That or "attacked by a raccoon."

As soon as we are in dry clothes we head to the one structure in the harbor: the bar. The handful of other sailors who also crossed through the rough water are easy to spot because of their thousand-yard stares and the fact that we are the ONLY patrons not yet drunk off our faces. Everyone else is in full buccaneer garb, using over-the-top "Argh, matey" accents and drunkenly groping what I hope are *their* wives. Debauchery is clearly best executed in a costume, and everyone seems to have forgotten this is real life. Alcohol might not be the best remedy for seasickness, but the inebriates are in markedly cheerier mental states, so we hurry to catch up.

We spend the night on the boat, and by eight the next morning, even through the thick hull, we hear the mating calls of functioning alcoholism. The sun is still low but the good people of Buccaneer Days are already up and harassing each other. Groups of aspiring marauders are piled in dinghies and weaving between the sailboats, throwing plastic coins and bellowing, "Prepare to be boarded!"

This is a lot. I'm not much of a morning drinker, but Luke has weed, so I gratefully smoke as much as he offers. It's like I'm at Mardi Gras but it's balding and in the middle of the ocean. I am getting a window into what it means to be an adult. Sometimes, being an adult means getting some friends together and whizzing around in a tiny boat shouting jocular threats at the passengers of slightly larger boats. It's quite a thing to watch grown men and women brandish fake swords and climb aboard the vessel you are standing on to demand beer. The environment (and probably the weed) bring me to a few surprising revelations:

1. People need escape and fantasy at every age.
2. Maybe we are all most free when we are playing make-believe.
3. At least five people here have buried a stripper in their lifetime.

My most pirate-y shirt happens to make my boobs look awesome, and twelve hours have passed since I last threw up, so I'm on the prowl. We get dressed and go ashore, and in the daylight I notice we are truly the only people here who are unmarried and under the age of fifty-five. Well, this changes everything. *Put me*

on an island with a cute guy and give him no other sexual options?
This must be how socially adept women feel all the time! I won't
even have to get that drunk! But I do anyway.

The next forty-eight hours are a haze. We dance, we take the
dinghy around the island, we drink more. We consume nothing
but overcooked mystery meat and the bar's signature drink: a
mixture of Kahlúa, Baileys, banana liqueur, and whipped cream
known as Buffalo Milk. The combination of sugar and alcohol
is probably shutting down vital organs, but we feel invincible.

On our last night, some of us go ashore for a last hurrah,
but Whitney and Brian stay on the boat to call it an early night.
Luke and I sneak away from the party and make out in the grass
under the stars. It would be romantic if we weren't dressed like
off-brand theme park entertainers.

I am drunk, and very young, and sharing a near-death experience makes me feel like I can say anything to Luke. I tell him
that watching Whitney and Brian stay on the boat made me de-
pressed. Then I say of course they stayed on the boat; why would
they bother coming out? Just to hang out with each other? Once
you're married there's no more excitement or possibility. I say
settling down sounds like death. I say I feel sorry for them.

I can't imagine anything more important than chasing that
"butterfly feeling." I can't imagine what would drive a person to
get out of bed in the morning if you knew you'd never have that
new-crush feeling again or ever dance on a table, or get so drunk
you try to fight a stranger. To not come ashore on the last night
of Buccaneer Days? It's tantamount to giving up on life.

Maybe because he's a little older, or maybe because Whitney is his sister, Luke scoffs. He's right; it's stupid. I just don't know it yet.

We get back on the boat and go to sleep. I bunk with Luke but we don't have sex after all because we haven't known each other very long, and his family is on the boat, and I haven't taken a shit since we left LA. The journey back is easy and beautiful. When we arrive in the marina everyone sets to work getting the boat back in order. Alex and I have no idea what to do but it seems like asking would slow the process down. We move objects around at random to give the appearance that we are helping. The second it becomes acceptable to say good-bye we run to my car, drive straight over a partition, and race home to the comfort of indoor plumbing. At home, we come out of our respective bathrooms, flop on the couch, and luxuriate in our freshly scrubbed bodies and vacant bowels.

For the first time in almost four days, we are sober on land. Did you know that land sickness is a thing? Spend too much time on a boat, and your body adjusts. We hadn't noticed it when we went ashore in Catalina because the only thing on that shore was alcohol. But now it starts to overtake us. I go to the kitchen thinking food will help and I am tossed about by invisible demons. My ten-foot walk to the refrigerator is perfectly flat but I flail and grab at the walls like I am traversing the galley of a sinking navy destroyer. Alex and I look at each other, terrified. Surely this is just a delayed hangover; it will be over in a few hours. But the ocean is an evil bitch and she intends to torture us for days. I crawl back to the bathroom and throw up.

• • •

Why would grown people do this?! These are adults with money—sailboat money! Which would imply they are functioning members of society! Why go to an island and dress up like a pirate? The *work* of it—the expense, the planning, the last-minute acquisition of stick-on Captain Jack Sparrow™ beards! All to come home and spend the next three days feeling miserable.

While I was there, I found this all bewildering but harmless. Yet I was undone by the simple act of husband and wife staying "in" one night in lieu of participating in what was clearly a collective psychosis.

Not long after that weekend, something started changing in me. I started to feel like I was just playing the part. The first time I noticed it I was in the middle of a herculean effort to enjoy dancing at a club in Vegas. Even while it was happening I thought, *This will be one of those things I look back on that makes me glad I don't do it anymore.* Later that night, Buccaneer Days crossed my mind. I still didn't know why anyone would want to go through all that trouble to behave like an idiot (to this day I behave like an idiot plenty and I don't need a pirate costume to do it), but I realized: I'd want to stay on the boat. I'd want to stay on the boat, cook some mystery meat, and listen to a podcast.

So many people I know who are in long-term relationships have made the same boring comment to me about how they wish Tinder had been around when they were single. Seriously, you wish you could be on Tinder? Tinder seems like a gateway to years of therapy or having your organs harvested. These comments are usually made by married men who feel that they would "clean up" if they could only get their incredible faces in front of the masses of younger women who "they've heard" are way more into anonymous sex.

So many people say they wish they could be young again. You couldn't drag me back to twenty-one. All the hiding, all the pretending, all the hanging out with people you don't actually like. Going out three nights in a row? *RuPaul's Drag Race* is on. Making out in the grass? I own a perfectly good couch. Always fighting with your friends? I am no longer confused about what the word "friend" means. And to top it all off, if you woke up tomorrow and you were young again, you'd have to deal with creepy married dudes feeling entitled to easy sex with you because your generation is supposed to be "more liberated." Pass.

That new-crush feeling? It just makes me tired. I thought that urgency, that need for the new experience, always thinking the next one might be better than the last, and the terror of potentially missing out on one, would be there forever.

These days, if my hair got fucked up in front of some cute boy I'd just think, *Hey, at least we're speeding up the inevitable. If you still want to spend some of your short time on earth with this whole situation, let me know, 'cause it's what you're gonna get at the end of the day.*

Pitying the couple who didn't want to semi-ironically hobnob with strangers in pirate costumes was pretty childish of me. But I'm glad I have the memory of that feeling, because now I can fully appreciate how wonderful it is that it's gone.

I wonder how much of my hard-and-fast worldview will change as I get older. Surely I will always hate licorice, I will always love cheap scented candles, and my favorite movie will always be George Cukor's *The Women*. Surely I will always put work before relationships, I will always think that children aren't for me, I will always find Buccaneer Days baffling. Or maybe in a few years I'll get the urge to sail to an island, spend the weekend getting hammered in a tricornered hat, and realize I was a fool for ever questioning it.

the world's most reluctant adult

I was in a rush to grow up my whole childhood. Because I looked so young as a kid, I worked doubly hard to prove that I was independent and mature. I got called "precocious" A LOT. I did not know the word had pejorative connotations until I grew up and started using it as code to mean *this kid is annoying* . . . and the circle was complete.

When I was nine, I bought a mini-fridge for my bedroom with my allowance money. It was fifty bucks at Walmart and I saved like a champ for my big purchase. I thought it would make me feel like I was living in a little apartment of my own. Instead, it sent me into a panic about all the things I would need to be a true adult: a microwave, a toaster, wooden hangers, a coffee

table, coffee table books, a little jar for cotton balls, a bike with hand brakes even though the pedal-backward-brake seemed perfectly fine to me, and a mop. (For our wall-to-wall carpeting? What was wrong with me?)

I returned the mini-fridge the next day. I felt like I either had to become a perfect adult human all at once, or give up and stay a kid. I let my anxiety get the better of me and chose to stick my head in the sand. I'm still doing battle with this anxiety and it's left me as a bit of a man-child. I know I'm not a man, but "woman-child" doesn't sound quite right. "Girl-baby"? "Lady-tyke"? I'm getting into creepy porno territory, so let's stick with man-child. You know what I mean anyway.

With every birthday, I have stupidly expected to feel different only to discover that I'm still me: tragically lazy and childish. Every birthday, I think this is the year I won't drown myself in store-bought cookie dough when I'm anxious about something. And every year I'm wrong.

Even as I write this I'm thinking, *Next year, though, it'll be better. The book will be done, I won't schedule myself so thin. I'll have enough time off to teach myself not to get overwhelmed.* And I really believe it! It's pathetic!

The truth is, I just want to be a man-child for another three months. Perpetually. Can you spot the tiny flaw in this mindset? I have no doubt that I'll need the help of a very skilled therapist to break this cycle, but I keep hoping it will correct itself. Every now and then I test the waters of self-improvement with some practical changes to see how far I can go without succumbing to anxiety. Just small things at first.

I stopped buying fancy underwear. Easy. I've bought so much of it in my life, and it turns out guys are way more excited about naked boobs than they are about boobs in a lacy red bra. Fancy bras are uncomfortable and look lumpy under anything I'd want to wear on a date anyway. Also, every time I've worn fancy lingerie, an awkward dance ensues where I try to pause in between the removal of the shirt and the removal of the bra, so that the gentleman might admire me. It's even worse with jeans and underwear. Trying to keep your adorable knickers on when peeling off skinny jeans is like trying to get a Reese's Peanut Butter Cup out of the wrapper without the bottom layer of chocolate coming off. I've come to my senses and it's white cotton comfort all the way. Bam. That wasn't so bad.

I'm also working on becoming the kind of adult who does not engage in stupid, dangerous situations, even if that makes me look uncool. You know those videos on YouTube of a flash flood where someone is way too close to the water and they're standing there like, *Wow, that water is rising fast. I'll just take a few more pictures and I'll totally be able to get out of here before I'm in any jeopardy*, and then they're DEAD! I want to be the person who runs away from the flash flood like a little bitch and lives to tell the tale. I am not going to be the person who shows off by leaning too far into the dolphin enclosure and then gets raped to death by dolphins (Google it, nerds). I'm going to be the person who tells her friends not to get too close to the dolphins, gets made fun of, and says "I told you so" at their funerals. I used to be the idiot who would climb to the fifth floor of a construction site at two a.m. just for the story. Now the most reckless thing I do is ignore emails marked urgent. It's a real rush.

I'm trying to make big decisions without asking "an adult." Because that's me. I'm the adult. For ten years I drove Charlie, my scrappy little used Toyota. When it came time to buy a new car, I decided to do it on my own. I'm financially stable, I am a homeowner, I vote, but I'll admit, it felt weird not consulting my parents. I'd bought Charlie when I was a teenager—I'd used my own money, but my mom was with me the whole time. I had no idea how to buy a car *completely* on my own. So I brought Aubrey Plaza. Aubrey's got kind of a father-figure vibe, so she gave me a certain confidence walking into the dealership.

Aubrey was accidentally helpful in the negotiation process, because she's batshit crazy. I was getting frustrated with the cliché trappings of the process and kept asking, "Do we really need to do this? You're going through the motions of being a sleazy used-car salesman, but couldn't we just talk like two normal humans?" Aubrey sat in the corner and occasionally interjected, "My uncle owns a dealership across town and we could just go there. He's also in the mafia," without looking up from her phone. We were less "good cop/bad cop" and more "cop who hates negotiating/cop having a psychotic break." The technique was effective regardless.

I went home and called my mom to tell her I'd bought a car. Maybe that kind of thing is newsworthy enough to warrant a call to your mom anyway, but my motivation was that of a child who'd learned to tie her shoe. What's the point of being so independent if you don't get a gold star from your mother for being such a big girl! Maybe the next time I buy a car I'll wait a week to call her. If my current track record holds up, I have until 2024 to develop that kind of restraint.

The further I get into self-improvement, the more I hope I'll grow some new part of my brain that makes me take care of my responsibilities automatically. Like highway blindness. If I grabbed my keys for a Krispy Kreme run in my sweatpants, I'd come to twenty minutes later, wearing pleated khakis and getting my oil changed. Sadly, I am conscious through every excruciating moment of paying my parking tickets on the DMV website and cleaning a little bit each day so it doesn't pile up on me. I expected to take an interest in my retirement plan, understanding general car maintenance, and doing my laundry on a schedule instead of three days *after* I ran out of underwear. But just thinking about that stuff makes me want to lie on the floor and eat packets of Easy Mac until I feel too swollen and turgid to do anything but dream up elaborate ways to murder everyone who says "life hack." I power through. I'm still an embarrassment to civilized society, but now I change the toilet paper roll instead of resting it vertically on top of the old one. There's hope.

The trickiest areas to improve are my fitness habits. When I work on them, it's great for a while because I don't feel so sluggish and I have fewer mood swings, but shitty because healthy food tastes gross. Naturally luminous, perfectly proportioned people are always full of helpful tips to set me on the right path. Oh, aloe vera water is the new chia seed? Cool, I'll just work up the reserve of self-loathing I'll need to choke down that spit-flavored miracle drink. Why don't I just eat powdered egg whites until I pass out? (Eesh, add "food issues" to the therapy list.)

When it comes to exercise, I'll start out slow—just an easy hike. The next day I'll be too sore to move but I'll say the reason I can't hike again for a few days is because my allergies (to sunlight and pain) are acting up. I don't know who I'm "saying" that to—obviously I don't invite anyone to witness these feeble attempts at physical activity. Being healthy is testing my commitment, but I'm feeling pretty good about my monthly dose of seeing-the-sky.

Then I have to make the bed, and that's where it all falls apart. I hate making the bed so much. Way more than I should. I can't make my bed without collapsing into a full-on existential crisis. *So you made the bed. It looks nice. But . . . you are just going to get BACK into bed tonight. Then you'll have to make it again tomorrow, and on and on and on and then you'll be dead.* And then I'll start thinking, *Well, why do any housework? Why do the dishes? You're just going to get them dirty again. Maybe you should start eating every meal with your hands, bent over the trash can. Why work to improve any area of your life when everything good that happens is going to require more and more maintenance?!*

Maybe giving up on this adulthood thing wouldn't be so bad. In movies and TV the man-child always has a moment of clarity and gets his act together for his wife or his baby, but what if I just didn't? What if I just kept returning the proverbial mini-fridge?

When I'm in full man-child mode, I sleep until ten, dopey and sweating, my only motivation to stand the promise of an ice-cream sandwich to start the day. The mid-morning sugar crash isn't a problem when my only objective is to sit as still as possible while watching *Naked and Afraid.* People might roll their eyes at me, but they're just jealous because their hearts-of-palm ceviche sucks. Sure, my muscles are atrophied, but stacking my dirty dishes in the sink and leaving them there has become a veritable game of high-stakes Jenga, so my physical dexterity really isn't in question at this point.

Food and housework aren't the real problem. The real problem is that I let anxiety cripple my relationships. I blame this paralysis on different things. It started as a money issue: I was too broke to go out. I didn't want to spend money I didn't have on dinners and drinks and the movies. I didn't want to invite anyone over, because my place was gross. Once I had an income, it became a time issue: I'm working too much to go out. Even when I do have a free day or two, there's this overwhelming guilt about planning anything recreational. *I haven't been to the dentist in a year and a half, but I'm gonna go to Lacy's party? Out of the question.* I mean, I still won't go to the dentist, but making fun plans would force me to *acknowledge* that I'm not going to go to the dentist.

I get that it's not a money issue or a time issue, it's just a me-being-a-malfunctioning-life-form issue. I think I need to become perfect all at once, so I keep getting overwhelmed and putting it off. I can't remember the last time that I didn't have something hanging over my head. There are usually about thirty to eighty things. Is that normal? Don't tell me. If it's not, I'm a jerk. If it is, that's super-depressing, and I know I'll just use "this is normal" as an excuse to procrastinate even more.

I know that feeling isn't unique to me. Yes, I'm away from home a lot and keep the hours of a meth-addicted puzzle enthusiast (it takes as long as it takes, okay?!), but everyone in the world feels like their inbox is growing faster than they can keep up, right? If there was just a little more time, or a little more money, or if you could just get through this one last rough patch, it would all be clear, it would all fall into place. It's an insatiable trap.

And YET, I always think, *This is my year.* This year I'm going to get my shit SO together that I'll always be able to see the solution to my problems. I'm going to get it so together that I'll never have to "get it together" again. It's like this Tyler Durden–style feeling that I'm so close. I'm so close to being a real person. I'm so close to making time for friends and family. I'm so close to being able to take out the trash without checking that none of my neighbors are outside because small talk makes me feel like the world is on fire. I'm so close to being wonderful.

Sometimes I get tough with myself. *You are unbelievable! Nut up and fix your problems! You come from a long line of poor Irish women who were perfectly self-sufficient, and by the way, they had like a million babies a year!*

Then I'll play good cop. *Hey, buddy, maybe you could just answer a couple emails today? The one from your insurance company doesn't seem too scary, and you don't want to go to jail for driving uninsured, do you? No, of course you don't. And you're making money now, maybe get a cleaning service to come by like once a month, no pressure, just so it doesn't start looking like a fucking episode of* Hoarders *in here, okay?*

But I fight back. *Balance? Moderation? Discipline? These are just the many names for "smug" used by the bitches who lie to us on their lifestyle blogs. That's right, Clean Food Cross Fit Mom1, I know you've got a pile of fun-size Almond Joys in your glove compartment. Now go sit in your driveway and eat your candy while masturbating to Tom Hardy like a real woman!* You can see how I would think emotional adulthood is right around the corner.

I'll just be a man-child for another three months. I swear.

scrappy little nobody

I don't want to brag—I realize my elite lifestyle and celebrity status might intimidate you—but my car has keyless entry. That's right. My little beauty just needs to sense my presence and, as long as I have my keys in my pocket, she opens up like a gross sexual metaphor that's demeaning to women. Meow.

When I go out of town and drive a rental car, sometimes I will approach it, keys in pocket, and pull on the handle of a locked door. Well. It's an embarrassing situation, to say the least. I'm forced to push a button on a clicker to enter my motor vehicle . . . like some pleb. (We've been hanging out long enough that it's cool for me to make jokes like that, right?) It is an embarrassing situation, because expecting my car door to magically be unlocked makes me feel like a little spoiled-idiot baby who doesn't remember a time when she had to insert a key into a lock to get into her car. *Wahh, why won't this open?!*

Every time this happens it reminds me how quickly we take formerly miraculous things for granted. No Uber? How did we get places before? No Wi-Fi on this flight? I might actually die of boredom. No navigation on my phone? So I have to print out directions from the internet? Or look at . . . one of those big paper things . . . is it pronounced "map" as in "cap" or "mape" as in "vape"?

I don't want to become complacent. Lazy is something I've always been, but complacent and entitled I want to avoid. When we made *Up in the Air*, George once said that actors have a bad habit of thinking that however well their career is going, it will only get better from there. Well, not me! I'm going to assume the world could collectively turn on me at any moment! I suppose I should try to find a balance, but that seems harder.

Film actors are treated like useless idiots, because we often are. But I started in theater, dammit! I used to sleep on the floor of the Port Authority at fourteen waiting for the bus home after traveling six hours to New York for one lousy audition! This was my dream! I don't want to get used to any of it! Now where is the chilled oxygen I ordered!

When I first moved to LA, I didn't have a TV, so I went to my one friend's apartment to watch the Oscars. It was the year that Charlize Theron won for *Monster*. I watched her walk down the red carpet while I ate my questionable bodega hot dog and imagined that she must have spent the previous three weeks being expertly massaged and manicured in preparation. This was the most important night of her career. (It probably wasn't, but I thought that at the time. The most important moment of her career was more likely a day on set, actually doing her job.) I assumed that a team of specialists were working around the clock to monitor her food intake, skin regime, and eyelash density.

When I was nominated, in the weeks leading up to the Oscars I thought, *Doesn't anybody care that I'm not going to the gym, and I'm falling asleep in my makeup every night, and I'm eating like Macaulay Culkin in the first thirty minutes of* Home Alone? *Isn't anyone going to stop me? When is my Charlize Theron team going to parachute in and tell me what to do here?*

I thought celebrities never had to take care of anything themselves. In fact, I'm still guilty of thinking this now. I look at anyone richer or more famous than me and think, *Well, yeah, if I had a team of assistants, a nutritionist, and a trainer, I'd have Justin Bieber's abs, too!*

The weird thing is not how much people interfere with your life, but how little. No one wants to be the person to tell a celebrity they need to watch what they eat, or cut down on the boozing, or maybe just see a good old-fashioned therapist. (Obviously I already know I need to see a therapist, you don't have to tell me.) For the most part I'm on my own. Well, I get LOTS of help when it comes to things I would gladly avoid, like showing up to junkets or putting on real clothes for those junkets. The people who sign my checks know that I'd be cool with skipping them altogether. They send a small army to make sure I do it. But when I need a ride to the doctor because I've gotten bronchitis for the eighth time in six months, I'm drinking a Red Bull and gettin' behind the wheel.

And you know what? That's good. It builds character. I never *want* to build character, it's fuckin' awful, but it keeps me from becoming reliant on other people. I don't want to be like Paris Hilton, telling some judge that I didn't know my license was suspended because somebody was supposed to read my mail for me. I want to tell a judge that I didn't know my license was suspended because I don't have my shit together, but at least that's how I've always been! My ineptitude is not the result of fame! It's part of my god-given personality!

I spoke to Colin Firth at a party once and before I shared an inappropriate story about watching *Bridget Jones's Diary* on Ambien, he told my boyfriend and me that a few weeks earlier he'd gotten a flat tire on a country road. It was a very charming, self-deprecating story about how silly he felt not knowing what to do, and how he took a deep breath and figured it out, because he refused to behave like some helpless celebrity. Quite unfairly, my boyfriend and I started to use "Colin Firth" as shorthand for freezing up in the face of a minor problem. "Sorry I'm late, baby, the air conditioner kept turning itself off all day and I had a bit of a Colin Firth moment."

Never is this truer than when I stay in a nice hotel. It's so fancy, it's so well-appointed, it's so pleased with itself for being the height of luxury that when I can't locate a power outlet in the first ninety seconds of looking, I get unreasonably distressed. When I stay in a Motel 6 in Sarasota, Florida, I'm perfectly comfortable. Can't find a mini-fridge stocked with sparkling water? Of course you can't, you're at a Motel 6. At the crappy motel, I know I have to count on myself. And despite all evidence to the contrary, I can rely on this ol' gal to come through in a pinch.

I want to keep it that way. I don't want to become helpless. Some people think it's weird or uncouth when I do normal things, but people who actually think things like *Ew, why is Anna Kendrick buying toilet paper, doesn't she have an assistant or something?* are the same people who would think, *She has an assistant buy her toilet paper? She's worse than a terrorist.* So those people can choke to death on their own miserable worldview. XO! Conversely, some people act like I'm a literal hero for completing the smallest tasks without assistance, and I *agree*. Someone get me a medal.

Recently, a very sweet teenage boy stopped me on the street in Brooklyn. He asked for a photo and said, "How are you just . . . walking?" He knew what he was asking didn't exactly make sense. I told him walking wasn't so bad but I'd consider hiring a rickshaw the next time I left the house. He laughed, but I still think part of him was surprised I was executing a basic human function on my own.

I want to be a real person, even if that person wasn't so great to begin with. I want to always be able to say, *Hey, I'm not incompetent because I got famous, I'm incompetent because I'm a pathetic waste of humanity.* But I'm not about to let it get any *worse*. I don't want to be the guy who has to call an assistant the next time I get a flat tire. I still don't know how to change the tire, but I do know how to call roadside assistance. And I'm not going to let myself turn into a recluse because I'm embarrassed to be seen outside the context of perfectly glamorous situations. So if I come into your local 7-Eleven with a gown hiked up around my knees, asking for directions to my own premiere because the GPS broke, be cool about it.

I recently had jury duty. It was the second time I'd been called to perform my civic duty since moving to California. When I told friends I was doing it, the majority of them balked. "They make celebrities do jury duty?" Um, we're just people, of course they do! (Yes, obviously I was hoping that being famous would get me out of jury duty. I wasn't going to be the dick who called someone up and said it, though.) I *did* ignore the notice for several months. I was shooting a movie out of state and worried that if I called to postpone they wouldn't let me. On the other hand, if I called once I got home and ~~lied~~ explained that I had only unearthed the summons upon my return, how mad could they be? Better to ask forgiveness than permission. I know, it's the logic of a fool who goes to jail for ignoring a jury summons. But it turns out I was right! I had my rambling apology/excuse locked and loaded, but they rescheduled me without asking for one.

I'll admit I wondered if I would run into any problems. I really do assume that most people won't know who I am, because in my experience, they don't. Still, I never know when I'm going to be a distraction . . . or when a municipal employee might offer to smuggle me out the back door in exchange for, say, a signed 8 x 10 glossy. No, but seriously, I didn't want to interrupt the noble pursuit of justice.

I reported to a downtown courthouse without incident. The only person who approached me was a young woman in a pink tracksuit. She said she liked me in that movie where the dude had cancer, and she liked how it was funny and he didn't die. I asked her if she'd served jury duty before and she said, "No, I'm not here for jury duty, I'm waiting to go into court." *I have a fan who might be a criminal! Or a falsely accused political dissident! Or an unorthodox lawyer! Well, realistically she's probably just some girl in a civil dispute . . . with her tyrannical landlord!* This was exciting.

The prospective jurors got called in for orientation and I said good-bye to my new friend the criminal/hero/citizen. There were probably a hundred people shuffling in, so I took a seat at the very back of the room. So far so good. We watched a video of former jurors talking about their "rewarding experience" with such forced enthusiasm that I suspect their loved ones were being held at gunpoint just off camera. Then a woman in a business suit and orthopedic shoes gave us a speech about how as long as there wasn't any nonsense, we'd get along fine. I was starting to feel so anonymous that I got that lovely, familiar "alone in a crowd" sensation. She continued, "There is no photography in the courthouse. Now, you might want to take a photo because maybe you see a famous attorney, or a famous defendant, or maybe . . ." She raised her hand and pointed to the back of the room. ". . . even a famous juror." *Was she pointing at me? Dude, for real, are you pointing at me?? I'm being so stealthy! I'm all the way in the back of the room! You said "no nonsense"! This is definitely "nonsense"!*

"Well"—she put her hand down—"I guess she's not gonna say anything, but . . . anyway, she's just a juror today, so don't bother her." *Lady! I was doing fine before you did that!* Luckily, the other jurors were paying about as much attention as plane passengers during in-flight safety announcements, so almost no one turned around.

The rest of the day we waited in the orientation room to find out if we'd be put on a case. I sat in a corner and read some Philip K. Dick and tried to be inconspicuous—and ate vegan for lunch because it turns out *Do Androids Dream of Electric Sheep?* is WAY more about empathy for animals than the *Blade Runner* movie. In spite of Whistleblower McGee, no one seemed to notice me.

I didn't end up on a trial that day—perhaps Whistleblower had spared me to atone for her earlier "nonsense" transgression—but outside of that, the only incident that reminded me I was famous was when a sweet older gentleman asked if I was reading my book for research, to be in the movie version.

"No, this is actually already a movie. They changed the title to *Blade Runner* but they made it in the eighties."

"Oh," he said, "I thought that Frenchman who did *Sicario* was remaking it. You know, the one who always works with Roger Deakins."

Oh shit, Grandpa. That'll teach me to underestimate a fellow Los Angeleno.

There are plenty of places in the world where I am correctly treated like I ain't shit. My personal favorite is my hometown. While I was in the middle of writing this, I went home to see my parents. I turned off my phone, stopped checking my email, and hung around Maine long enough that I pushed through the awkward small-talk phase with my dad and managed to get him talking about Sergei Prokofiev fleeing Stalin's regime, which is his version of deep chat. I slept on my mom's sofa even though she kept offering to make up the bed in the basement, because I liked waking up to bright snowy mornings. We took long walks around her neighborhood, each time stopping by her favorite neighbor's house to say hello. The two young boys whom she often babysits were always thrilled to see her and could not have been less interested in me. It felt like how the world should be.

Being around my family and the place I grew up reminded me of my fear that I was getting too comfortable, that I was letting myself atrophy. When the apocalypse comes, my total lack of practical use in the world will make me a first-round draft pick to be cannibalized. How did I become so useless? Everyone else in my family is resourceful, brilliant, a problem solver by nature. I recently tried to kill a spider by chasing it around with a saucepan. There are several holes in my bedroom wall now. The spider lives on. You see what I mean?

During the visit I went through some childhood photos. After four shoeboxes of winter camping and historical fort pics (I didn't find out until I moved away from home that other families went to Disneyland for vacation), I found this little doozy.

This picture proved that my entire personality was fully formed by the time I was three. I was an obstinate, determined little ball of anxiety.

I'd thought of myself as fearful and shrinking in childhood, but I was often single-minded and pugnacious. From age three onward I have been practical and skeptical and occasionally more courageous than I have any right to be. At age three I'd decided those were the tools I needed to get through this life in one piece, and those tools aren't going away.

It was a wonderful discovery. It would make me so sad if naturally happy, open, kind children could be changed by their experiences and lose those qualities. My particular personality traits seem less worthy of preservation, but they are my own and I love them. I hate them a lot, too, but I can rely on them.

I shouldn't be so worried about "changing" as an adult. As an adult you get to turn to your boyfriend and say things like "I've always found the obligation to say 'god bless you' after a sneeze really arbitrary and mannered. When we're at home, can we stop saying it?" And then you get to stop! You have all this agency! You get to decide what kind of a person you want to be! And yet, you are still the person you were at three years old. Isn't that kind of great? I think three-year-old you would be proud.

I put that picture on my desk so that when I feel sorry for myself, her fearsome little face will be staring at me, saying, "Get off your ass and fight, woman!" I rarely give advice—your personal growth will only make me look worse by comparison—but as a *suggestion*, find your most psychotic baby picture and have it on hand for those days when you want to throw in the towel. It is both joyful and effective.

I hope that you have found this entertaining and maybe (my highest goal) it has made you feel less alone. If we ever cross paths I hope you have a good experience. I will try to be open and not squirrelly. I can't promise I'll be nice because nice isn't really who I am. Pygmy ferret cornered and ready for a fight is more like it.*†

---

* I wanted to put more shit talk in here but I figured I should be diplomatic since I'd like to continue working for at least a few more months. I'll write another book when I'm seventy. A better woman might let go of past conflicts, but don't worry, I hold a grudge forever. This has been fun. X

† Oh man. Is my Wikipedia page going to say "author" now? That's gonna make me look like such a dick.

bonus reading group guide

Welcome to the completely real and very serious reading group guide for the magnificent book *Scrappy Little Nobody*. Below are a few questions to help you get the most out of your reading experience.*

Book club meetings should commence with an interpretative dance based on your emotional journey through the book. Refreshments (preferably a variety of Pop-Tarts and a dry prosecco to be drunk from the bottle) should be served liberally throughout the proceedings. We hope these discussion points aid the further appreciation of the material you've just read.

1. Though every page of *Scrappy Little Nobody* is perfect in every way, which part is your favorite? Make a list (it can just be a Post-it that says "Every part is my favorite") and tape it to your chest for the rest of the day.

---

* If you happen to run a trashy celebrity news blog that requires you to peruse the content of privileged cretins like me, first of all I'm sorry, and second, you may use these questions as a template for creating misleading but juicy headlines. BTW, I get it, famous white girls are really fun to be mad at.

2. Discuss the metaphor of Anna moving to Los Angeles without a motor vehicle. Was this an illustration of her tendency to self-sabotage, or did she just not look at a map of the city before she moved, like an idiot?

3. Why do you think Anna chose to disclose her childhood affiliation with the KKK? Was the guilt finally too much for her? Or is she trying to make white supremacy feel accessible and fun for a new generation?

4. When Anna compares Zac Efron to Charles Manson, is she making a joke or trying to warn us about a potential murderous mastermind?

5. Does Anna hate all Russians or just the one man who teased her about her name? Does her xenophobia stem from this experience or simply being raised in the era when all bad guys in movies were Russian?

6. The book opens with the author's mother wishing for a few stories in which Anna comes across as thoughtful and/or generous. Did Anna's mother get her wish? Was there a single story where Anna didn't seem eminently punchable?

7. In the section about Alexa Chung and Olivia Palermo, the author viciously maligns two innocent and very fashionable girls. Is Anna a shady, basic bitch, or the shadiest, basic-est bitch?

8. What was up with that one chapter about sailing being in the present tense? Sure, Anna's editor thought that was weird, but it's what Anna wanted.

Who was right? The pigheaded author or the noble (and very pretty) editor?

9. Did Anna steal that money from her neighbor's pizza party? Did she include the story to hide her crime in plain sight? Let's petition to get her tax returns released and finally take this bitch down!

10. Why does Anna want to engage in a Valentine's Day orgy? Is she simply desperate for human contact or does she not understand acceptable social boundaries?

11. Anna makes a lot of bad decisions. Can you think of a time when you've made a bad decision? Oh wow, really? We're gonna pretend you can't think of a single example? YOU THINK YOU'RE BETTER THAN ME?!

acknowledgments

I would like to gratefully thank: Jeff Blitz for lending your brain and for throwing cake at me. Georgia Stitt for your musical guidance. Kay Cannon for keeping me honest. Cait Hoyt for your warmth and support. Lauren Spiegel, my literary sherpa, thank you for your patience and for occasionally letting me win.

about the author

Anna Kendrick is shorter in person.